JN411081

Selected Issues on the Russian Arctic Circle:

Society, Culture, Economy and Law

Selected Issues on the Russian Arctic Circle:

Society, Culture, Economy and Law

Wooik Choi

Seungdo Ra

Bongchul Kim

Ho Kim

Minkyung Shin

Preface

There are more than one definition of the so-called, 'Arctic Circle,' which firstly refers to the area upper 66-degree north latitude. It could also denote a long borderline that geographically divides the polar region and the temperate climate region in the Northern Hemisphere. This boundary is also the criterion for the summer solstice and the winter solstice at the same time, and during the summer time the white night, where sun does not fall below the horizon, is continued. Accordingly, another definition of the Circle simply refers to the latitude where white night goes on. However, generally, the term is used as a name for the northern high latitudes, which is centred by the pole.

Although the Circle area has long been a place where human power cannot reach, it has also been a place where mankind constantly challenged despite the immense expense. These days, in response to the international political and economic situation of the modern society, this region is unprecedentedly drawing attention of many. In particular, environmental changes, such as global warming, dramatically increased the likelihood of further development in the Arctic, and many neighboring countries are attempting to explore and develop the natural resources of the area.

As the Arctic Circle has new economic development opportunities, including the use of resource development and route, it is currently attracting a worldwide attention. In 1989, the countries adjacent to the Arctic started the discussions for conservation of the North Pole environment, and in 1991, they established the organization 'Arctic Environment Protection Strategy (AEPS).' These efforts are continued by the 'Arctic Council,' which is established for the inter-governments' consultation on the sustainable development within the Arctic region. All Arctic countries joined the Arctic Council, which is more like a forum, in 1996 through the 'Ottawa Declaration.' At present, the Arctic Council is undertaking multiple collaborative operations with various international organizations, as well as with observer countries.

Russia has recently been pushing hard several projects to develop new routes and underground resources in the Arctic Circle area. The development and the influx of modern technology have sparked a change in the natural environment and traditional culture of the surrounding region, triggering a crisis in indigenous people's way of survival. Therefore, the Russian Federation and local governments are looking for sustainable development methods to solve the problems of the region. Korea and Russia are constantly making progress toward sharing economic benefits through joint projects for resource development and searching for diverse economic cooperation methods, not only confined to simple commodity trades. They are looking forward to achieving development of the Russian Arctic Circle, which is anticipated a prospective marketability.

The Polar Research Center at Hankuk University of Foreign Studies (HUFS) has been continuously conducting research on the Arctic Circle area of Russia. This book is an extension of the study with the supports from the Polar Academic Program (PE20900) of the Korea Polar Research Institute. The topics of this book cover the socio-cultural changes and conservation issues, which are mainly related to the economic development potential of the Arctic region, and suggest remedies and problem-solving measures using laws and systems. The four research works in this book are mainly modified and developed from the previous articles and papers of the authors.

A huge contribution of many has assisted the publication of this book. We would like to pay tributes to Dr. Hyuk Jeong, Senior Researcher, and Ms. Yangkyeong Lee, Ms. Kristina Vasileva, Ms. Kamila Almetova, Ms. Eunbee Cho, Ms. Sungryoung Park and

Ms. Gulzhanar Khairolla who are the assistants at the HUFS Polar Research Center. Also, the publication of this book would not have been possible without the efforts and support of the Knowledge Contents & Press at HUFS. Finally, we would like to clearly note that all studies have been based on many supports of the partner researchers in Korea and Russia regarding the project.

The Authors, 2020

Contents

The Prospect of the Legal Infrastructure for the Korea-Russia Trade:

Focusing on the Arctic Sea Route Cooperation

Bongchul Kim & Ho Kim

I. Introduction

The Arctic Circle area has long remained beyond human power. Nevertheless, the potential for development is growing due to environmental changes: such as the global warming. Meanwhile, Russia, which is most close to the Circle, is actively delivering a number of projects to develop new routes as well as oil and gas resources in the region. The country still continues to take aggressive measures, including the plan to set up the so-called "Ministry for the Development of the Russian Far East and Arctic" as in the federal level. (Staalesen 2019)

This situation is affected by the globalization of the international economy, and the communities are also connected to many variables. In fact, the Arctic communities of Russia are undergoing a variety of changes to date due to industrial development, and it is facing difficult challenges as well. The development and the influx of modern civilization are causing changes accordingly, in the natural environment and traditional culture which bring direct impact on the minority indigenous people within the region, and are triggering crises in their way of survival. The international community is seeking for sustainable development methods that involve considerable attention and effort to preserve the Arctic Circle. (Zadorin, Klisheva, Vezhlivtseva & Antufieva 2017, 4-5)

Seeing through the history, the earnest economic cooperation between Korea and Russia began in the early 1990s, along with changes in diplomatic ties and systems with the former Soviet Union. Currently, two countries are constantly developing the situation to share economic benefits through joint projects for resource development and explore diverse economic cooperation methods, not only staying within a simple commodity trade. In particular, as Russian federal government imply economic significance to Far East-Siberian region, attempt to provide support and development in this area could also be a major turning point for Korea-Russia economic cooperation.

Due to global warming, the possibility of developing Arctic shipping routes has become realistic as glaciers in the Arctic have gone smaller. Accordingly, as the interest for Korean companies has rapidly increased, the related research targets are also converging on the development of the shipping routes and the establishment of global logistics networks. Researches regarding development and utilization of the Russian Arctic Circle and its resources, and expansion of Arctic routes and logistics routes are already underway in Korea. This trend is accelerating, especially in conjunction with Korean government's 'New Northern Policy.' Nevertheless, so far most of the domestic research achievements are short-term proposals, taking into account policies and political situations of the countries.

International legislation related to the development of the Arctic Circle has steadily expanded its scope of discipline. Russia has a duty to respect and abide by international law regarding the development of the area. At the same time, the Russian government is also showing signs of strengthening domestic legal discipline based on the standards of international law. However, the country still sometimes offers different opinions from the international community's concern related to the development of the region after the economic sanctions and fails to avoid conflicts with other countries in terms of policies and institutions.

In this context, in order to expand exchanges between Korea and Russia related to the development of the area, it is essential to look at the conflict of the system from a legal point of view. It is of interest to establish a new bilateral normative system to avoid confrontations, which are specified to this issue. This paper looks at international and domestic legal discourses that may be relevant to the development of the Russian Arctic Circle and seeks to derive legal challenges that could be discussed in the future, such as in the Korea-Russia FTA.

II. Russia's Development of the Arctic Circle and Korea's Possibility for Participation

1. Development of the Arctic Circle in Russia

From Russia's point of view, the economic value of this particular region is enormous, that the Arctic can be considered as the stepping stone to overcome difficulties, such as international economic sanctions. (Kim 2017, 51-52) Furthermore, this area can provide Russia benefits in many aspects, including its national security, politics, military, technology, and environment, beyond the mere economic perspective of the region as a hub of resources. The Russian government is making great efforts for economic development while securing security awareness of the Arctic Circle. (Seidler 2010, 258)

The potential for development in this area ranges widely from the tourism industry to the large-scale resource exploitation. As each of these possibilities are closely linked to one another, Russia is keen on locating areas where its potential synergies lie in. For example, it is fully predictable that the development of resources in the Arctic Circle will accelerate further exploration of the Arctic route. Russia is showing high interest in developing resources that are not in the economic sanction list. Moreover, the exploration and utilization of the so-called Arctic route across the regional ocean is recently receiving massive attention along with the climate change.

Russia is being quite active in improving the innovative systems regarding the development and preservation of the Arctic Circle. Its move to introduce the 4th industrial revolution technology in the Arctic cities and to build smart cities can be one of the representative cases. At the federal level, Russia has steadily tried to forge partnerships with foreign companies and to implement advanced technologies with the aim of the sustainable development of the Arctic Circle. Russia, for instance, has already begun building Smart City Systems in certain cities, including Vladivostok by introducing technology from Japan. Of course, it will take considerable time and effort to realize visible achievements throughout Russia's entire Arctic Circle, but in the long run, the Russian government is anticipating to phase the smart city systems in the population dropping areas.

With regard to the development of the Arctic Circle, the global interest in so-called Northern Sea Route (NSR) that runs through the Arctic Ocean, is also growing significantly. The NSR can be distinguished into the northwest one in the Canadian waters, linking North America and Europe, and the northeast one in Russian waters which links Asia and Europe. (Yun 2009, 55) The Northeast route, especially, has the advantage that 1), is geographically shorter than the generally used current route, which connects East Asia and Europe through the Suez Canal and 2). Accordingly, it is able to greatly reduce the sailing days and logistics costs. (Humpert & Raspotnik 2012, 281-283) In Korean context, it is also possible that the route will revolutionize the global logistics system if it is well settled, where it is able to cut the operating hours by up to half from Busan to Europe.

Recently, the use of the routes for economic purposes has gained attention with the global warming due to climate change, the development of science, communication, and shipbuilding technologies, and the growing demand for logistics as the development goes on in the Arctic Circle. In particular, the use of NSR is expected to expand significantly as the climate change affected glaciers are shrinking and ice-breaking technology is developing. Therefore, many countries are using the route in a dramatic manner. (Park 2016, 29-30) Korea explored the Arctic route as well with the research purpose icebreaker *Araon* and now continues to build foundation for its commercial use.

Antarctica is the land that does not belong to any country under international law and is known as *Terrae Nulius*. However, the Arctic Circle is home to countries such as Russia and Canada. Therefore, when ships pass through the Arctic Ocean, consents from these countries are important. The Arctic Ocean however faces difficulties such as, since it is frozen even in the summer, sailing in this area definitely requires icebreakers, and especially in the winter time, the sailing speed has to be maintained at extremely low velocity. Because even icebreakers are not enough for ships to follow the route, newly designed vessels are needed. There are still unknown risks for navigation, weather, and so on as accurate data is hard to collect.

A case in point related to the development of Arctic Circle and Arctic Route is the 'Yamal LNG (Liquefied Natural Gas) Project' invested by France and China for a further step in Yamal Peninsula, Russia. The region has reserves of about 2.5 billion tons of oil and 3.5 billion tons of gas. The core of the project is to build logistic bases to transport the exploited resources to Europe and Far East Asia region. The copper mines in the Chukotka area and the construction of the Kamchatka LNG transshipment terminal are also linked to such projects. (Hodges, Shiryaevskaya & Khrennikova, 2018)

2. Potential for Growth of the Arctic Development related Industries

The development of the Arctic Circle will provide opportunities for related industries to grow together. For example, resource exploitation remains as a highly anticipated area despite concerns that it will create several environmental problems. Especially, the Plant market with direct links to the resource exploitation is growing rapidly. The Russian Plant market, which stood at around $8.2 billion in 2000, had grown up to $15.8 billion in 2010, nearly double the figure in a decade. The attraction power of the Russian Plant market comes from the possibility of combining the orders for plants with Korea's resource development.

Heavy Industries department of Samsung has supplied Sakhalin with the world's largest 33 story ocean platform "Runsko-A," and has won orders for three 70 million tons of icebreaker for the Arctic shipping line from Russia's largest state-run shipping company Sovcomflot. Daewoo Shipbuilding & Marine Engineering also participated in a project to modernize 'Zvezda dockyard,' which is under Russia's state-run shipbuilding group 'United Shipbuilding Co.,' located in the Bolshoi Kamen area near Vladivostok. Daewoo Shipbuilding & Marine Engineering is co-participating in the process of manufacturing LNG tankers, floating plants, and drilling vessels. The company won all 15 orders for the first "Yamal Project" in 2014, which is worth a total of $4.8 billion.

This basically means that Korea's technology has opened the era of full-fledged LNG transportation to the Arctic and touched off for energy development in the region. For Russia, it has also been a trigger to have confidence in the development of Arctic energy and transport through the route. It is meaningful that the Yamal LNG project is carried out with the participation and support from foreign countries not only with Russia's own labor force, but also sustainably maintained under the economic sanctions. The project created momentum for Russia's development of the Arctic Circle, and gave Korea the motivation to participate in. (Kim 2017, 51-52)

The Russian government's interest in building smart cities in the Arctic region gives evidence for predicting the potential growth of related industries. This, of course, is fully linked to the companies' possibilities to participate. Many Korean companies already have information and communication technologies, along with accumulated experiences of applying them to smart city constructions. These related experiences by the companies are properly reflected in overseas construction sites, resulting successful smart city cases overseas.

However, in order to succeed, we need to prepare for the limitations of this possibility. In particular, in the Far East Russia region, there are major limitations for companies to operate finances through foreign exchange control, which includes the friction between the central and local governments, excessive tax investigations, environmental regulations, and control of remittance to overseas. There is also the risk of unannounced policy changes or tax and environmental investigation on companies, causing them to go bankrupt even though they are still in the black. The Korean government and companies must have sufficient risk management and capital procurement capabilities in common, in advance.

The Russian government and society, however, have several challenges on the development of the Arctic Circle. For example, in the Arctic region there are ethnic minorities who have long lived on the ground, where the jurisdiction of the Russian federal government could not reach deep enough. These people are considerably vulnerable to changes in the environment and society following regional development. The challenges to care or control them internally are complicated tasks to find solutions even at the Russian Federation level.

These problems are manifested in a variety of forms, for instance, discrimination or prejudice against minorities, excessive involvement of central and local governments or abuse of power, conflict with migrant workers, language and cultural maladjustment, and lack of education and social participation. In response, the Russian government has established a number of legal systems, such as the Constitution and the federal or local level laws, as well as the policies and systems for carrying them out. From the international perspective, it is also making efforts to match the international standards.

On the other hand, the reality is that the preparation or implementation of these policies is still unsatisfactory and further improvement is needed. In one aspect, the complex composition of Russian society is the cause of the problem and it often has to be resolved within the society, but from another angle, encourage inter-governmental cooperation to carry out common opinions in the international community, enterprises' social contribution, or cooperation with non-governmental organizations and others can be a win-win solution.

In terms of cooperation with the international community, sometimes the appropriate cooperation with the third countries, such as Korea, provides a clue to solving these complex internal problems. Of course, for now, the idea that Russia will solve its own problems in cooperation with the outside world might sound a bit infeasible, and that such efforts could also be an ambiguous or abstract in long-term perspective. Nevertheless, in the process of establishing Korea-Russia economic cooperation and the excavation of new industries, there will be the possibility of bilateral policy cooperation, or at least to extract the momentum of new industries.

3. Cooperation Possibility between Korea and Russia on the Arctic Route

As the development of the Arctic Circle goes active in the close future, it will ratchet the demand for ships and equipment up, which are needed for exploration and navigation of the route and mining, transport and storage of resources. Therefore, while investing in the development of related new materials and core technologies, Korea should attempt to hold joint research with Russian institutes and sustain the exchange. The climate change in the area and the deteriorated facilities are putting Russia's port infrastructure in urgent need. Approaching from the other side, it can be an opportunity for the Northeast Asian country to eagerly participate in modernizing the ports, reflecting the its own port development technology. (Jeh and Min 2014, 1-6)

The NSR has been commercially used in near 2010, which steadily increased the frequency from 41 times in 2011, 46 times in 2012, to 71 times in 2013. In 2017, 10.7 million tons of cargo were transported via the route, and even the 2018, the summer ship *Maersk* succeeded in navigating the first container ship, *Venta Maersk*, through the sea route without the assist of an icebreaker. Based on this route, *Maersk* has been considering to utilize this route through cooperating with a Russian icebreaker, however, it is still on the examination process of possible sailing days and the rising costs for breaking additional ice. (Baker 2019)

Bulk cargo is likely to be used early in the use of Arctic shipping routes, as long as the transport conditions are simple and the demands for specific goods are adequate. In the future, a direct transport demand for Arctic shipping routes to Northeast Asia will be generated in accordance with the exploitation of resources in the Arctic region, and natural gas and oil could flow in large scales into Japan, Korea and Taiwan through these routes. However, it is a mid-long-term consideration, since the typical container transport can only be carried out if it is maintained sustainably. The global container shipping market is forming an economy of scale due to the growing size of ships. However, in the case of Arctic shipping routes, it is difficult to actually realize the economy of scale, because of the limited number of ships. Furthermore, as there is still a high risk, the economic feasibility is low due to the high insurance premium and navigation fee. (Park & Lee 2015, 244)

In 2010, the Korean government launched 'Eurasia Initiative Project,' which encompasses Russia and Central Asia, as a way to unite the Eurasian continent into a single economic community and to build peace on the Korean Peninsula by inducing openness to North Korea. The Korea's domestic interest in Russian Arctic region and Arctic routes has also increased in the context of this project. In particular, as the climate change accelerates, Korea is planning to expand logistic networks using sea routes by exploring the Arctic routes. In the case of land routes, it takes a considerable amount of time due to the railroad and the agreement between countries to transport, compared to the advantages of the sea route.

In terms of pioneering the Arctic route, the Korean government paying attention on linking the ports in Russia's Far East area. It aims to connect Korean ports to the Arctic routes, continental railways, and the Russia's Far East ports in a bid to strengthen its logistics and energy network. The main reason that the government was focusing on the marine aspect was because the logistics market was mostly through the port. Given that the Eurasian logistics market accounts for about 28% of the worldwide logistics market, and that it is growing more than 11% annually, it is quite spontaneous that the region becomes the target of attention.

In September 2013, Hyundai Glovis succeeded in commercial pilot sailing of the Arctic route for the first time in Korea. In addition, the Korean government prepared the basis for reducing fees for using port facilities from January 2014 and attempted to expand infrastructure, including the personnel trainings for sailing in polar areas. Currently, there are a number of domestic studies going on, including the ones from Korea Polar Research Institute (KOPRI). Furthermore, in addition to the studies in science and technology, topics in the humanities and social sciences have been conducted recently. Through these studies, Korea will be able to analyze the various existing problems within the commercialization of Arctic routes and eventually find the solutions.

III. Legal Obstacles with Russian Arctic Circle Development

1. International and Russian Domestic Regulation for Arctic Circle: Focus on the Regulations on the Arctic Routes

The international legal issues in traditional aspect, the region was mainly put on the table for the sake of sovereignty, rights, and jurisdiction of coastal countries. The international regulations have affected the enactment and application of domestic laws in the related countries. For example, the United Nations Convention on the Law of the Sea (UNCLOS) does not have specific provisions for the Arctic Ocean itself, but the provisions of Article 234 on 'Ice-covered areas' provide the basic principles for environmental protection and conservation applicable to the Arctic Ocean.

UNCLOS, Article 234 (Ice-covered areas) Coastal States have the right to adopt and enforce non-discriminatory laws and regulations for the prevention, reduction and control of marine pollution from vessels in ice-covered areas within the limits of the exclusive economic zone, where particularly severe climatic conditions and the presence of ice covering such areas for most of the year create obstructions or exceptional hazards to navigation, and pollution of the marine environment could cause major harm to or irreversible disturbance of the ecological balance. Such laws and regulations shall have due regard to navigation and the protection and preservation of the marine environment based on the best available scientific evidence.

According to this Article, measurement such as the enactment of a domestic law for the purpose of necessary control by the coastal countries of the Arctic Ocean can be undertaken, if there is or it is considered that any damage or such concern regarding the marine environmental pollution or the navigation of ships in frozen waters occurs. In fact, coastal countries have already prepared and applied various domestic laws on ship unloading, safety, design, installation, and navigation notices based in this context. However, there is a limitation that the domestic law should have appropriate boundaries and scientific grounds. After all, the international law serves to set the limits, at the same time providing a basis for the preparation of domestic laws for the countries.

As Russia is the one which has the most access to the Arctic Ocean, and especially since a large portion of the Arctic route has to pass through the Russian coast, ensuring maritime security is vital to the country's economy and is also of strategic importance. Russia has prepared and enforced domestic laws based on such international laws. (Rho & Park 2011, 97-121) The 2012 Federal Law of Shipping on the Water Area of the NSR amended in certain respects the 1998 Federal Act on Coastal Waters as well as the 1999 Marchant Shipping Code of the Russian Federation.

The federal law describes the NSR as 'historically developed national transport communication of the Russian Federation.' Any navigation by vessels in the Russian NSR is to be organized on an approval and remuneration basis, subject to compliance with specific rules for such navigation. Then, Rules of Navigation in the Water Area of the NSR was approved by the order of the Ministry of Transport of Russia in 2013. Based on the domestic laws, 'The Northern Sea Route Administration' was established as a federal state institution. According to the Russian government, the main targets of the institution are ensuring safe navigation and protection of marine environment from the pollution in the water area of the NSR.

The laws cover all vessels that pass through the Russian Arctic routes and the vessels are subject to the application regardless of their country. The laws allow the Russian government to adjust the shipping operations in consideration of weather conditions on the routes. The ship operators or captains who wish to pass through the Russian NSR must notify the type and duration of operation to the maritime operations headquarters and apply to use the respective route. Russia also prohibited ships that did not carry the 'letter of financial ship-owner's guarantee' on board, as part of its civil liability for environmental pollution in the Arctic coast and the vicinity of the sea.

Under the laws, the ships that use Arctic must meet the requirements and the captain and his agent must also have experience in operating ships in the ice zone. Russian authorities may conduct a crackdown inspection in the event that ships operating on the Arctic route are brining risk for sea or for pollution. Furthermore, it is mandatory to carry the 'Ice pilot' in certain waters. For a foreign warship to operate the Arctic route, a sailing plan, including the name of the warship and the captain, the purpose of the operation and the expected route and timing, must be submitted to the Russian government 45 days in advance. In the event of maritime accidents or pollution of the marine environment, there is also a clause which states that a Russian pilot must board the ship in order to deliver information to a nearby Russian port or naval base and to ensure the safety of the ship. Even if, however, the ship met all the above requirements, the Russian government can always refuse the operation of a foreign warship in the Arctic route without prior notice, and it also has the authority to take military emergency measures.

The Russian laws regarding the Arctic routes has brought controversies, that it is too restrictive beyond the standards of international law. Furthermore, some are pointing out whether Russia has the authority to apply the approval system for the ships that are exempt from sovereignty. The logic of this criticism is that although the Russian government claims the domestic law was enacted to protect the environment and shipping activities based on UNCLOS Article 234, foreign warships subject to this regulation are excluded from the application of UNCLOS Article 234. The following UNCLOS Article 236 concerns sovereign-exempt ships that are excluded from the application of the Article 234.

UNCLOS, Article 236 (sovereign immunity) The provisions of this Convention regarding the protection and preservation of the marine environment do not apply to any warship, naval auxiliary, other vessels or aircraft owned or operated by a State and used, for the time being, only on government non-commercial service. However, each State shall ensure, by the adoption of appropriate measures not impairing operations or operational capabilities of such vessels or aircraft owned or operated by it, that such vessels or aircraft act in a manner consistent, so far as is reasonable and practicable, with this Convention.

If Korea and Russia sustainably cooperate on the Arctic development, both might be able to make legal co-suggestions to the international society in case of necessity. For example, there is no general international law yet to discipline the responsibility for pollution or damage, even though the marine plants for resource exploitation, like ships, are at risk of leakage accidents and pollution. These problems are simply being solved only by the voluntary agreement between the domestic laws of respective countries, regional cooperative arrangements, or the operators of offshore plants. Seoul and Moscow could consider proposing general norms to the international community, along with signing a bilateral agreement between the two.

2. Necessity of a New Legal Foundation for the Economic Cooperation

Korea and Russia have often joined together in expanding multilateral treaties on the international stage while continuing their efforts on economic cooperation since the establishment of diplomatic ties. At the same time, the two partners signed bilateral treaties for continuing their direct cooperation. These treaties are mainly for investment, resource exploitation, transport, and etc., but also include promises of military and security. The major bilateral treaties signed between two since 2000 are as follows.

Agreement between the Government of the Republic of Korea and the Government of the Russian Federation on Cooperation in the Fields of Energy (2000)
Agreement between the Government of the Republic of Korea and the Government of the Russian Federation on the Mutual Protection of Classified Military Information (2001)
Agreement between the Government of the Republic of Korea and the Government of the Russian Federation on the Prevention of Dangerous Military Activities (2003)
Agreement between the Government of the Republic of Korea and the Government of the Russian Federation on Cooperation on the Program of the Medium Range Surface-to-air Missile System (2005)
Air Service Agreement between the Government of the Republic of Korea and the Government of the Russian Federation (2003)
Agreement between the Government of the Republic of Korea and the Government of the Russian Federation on Cooperation in the Gas Industry (2006)
Agreement between the Government of the Republic of Korea and the Government of the Russian Federation on Technology Safeguards Associated with Cooperation in the Field of the Exploration and Use of Outer Space for Peaceful Purpose / Protocol to the Agreement between the Government of the Republic of Korea and the Government of the Russian Federation on Technology Safeguards Associated with Cooperation in the Field of the Exploration and Use of Outer Space for Peaceful Purpose of 17

October 2006 (2006)

Agreement between the Government of the Republic of Korea and the Government of the Russian Federation on Cooperation in Preventing Illegal, Unreported and Unregulated Fishing of Living Marine Resources (2009)

Agreement between the Government of the Republic of Korea and the Government of the Russian Federation on Temporary Labor Activities of Citizens of One State in the Territory of the Other State (2010)

Agreement between the Government of the Republic of Korea and the Government of the Russian Federation on Marine Transport (2010)

Agreement between the Government of the Republic of Korea and the Government of the Russian Federation on the Mutual Abolition of Visa Requirements (2013)

Agreement between the Government of the Republic of Korea and the Government of the Russian Federation on the Establishment and Operation of Cultural Centers (2013)

Agreement between the Government of the Republic of Korea and the Government of the Russian Federation on Cooperation in the Field of Maritime Search and Rescue (2016)

Agreement between the Government of the Republic of Korea and the Government of the Russian Federation on the Establishment of the Direct Secure Communication System (2017)

Bilateral treaties between the two partners, signed since the 1990s, have largely provided disciplines on the cooperation. Among them, such treaties as the ‘Agreement between the Government of the Republic of Korea and the Government of Russian Federation on Economic Cooperation in the Republic of Sakha (Yakutia) 1995’ cover areas of the Arctic Circle. The treaties also create new usability with the recent Arctic region issues. The legal infrastructure for realizing a new level of cooperation is also necessary to consolidate and harmonize various bilateral agreements that have been signed so far to discipline various areas of the cooperation. (Kim 2015, 421)

Now we need to pay attention to the previous Free Trade Agreement (FTA) that it has signed between Korea and many other countries. The FTA promises to remove trade barriers, including tariffs on trade between signatories, while the latest deal calls for the removal of passive trade barriers, as well as providing special trade benefits to the partner. In the end, the FTA has become the most leveraged legal base among various international economic treaties, which most WTO member countries also are using as well. FTA signatories are now fully committed to its original purpose – to provide special trade benefits for the economic sake of the partner, however, they are also used for non-economic purposes. In such cases, the FTA serves to broaden the areas of cooperation between the countries concerned and can be used for various other purposes. (Kim 2018, 79)

Korea is focusing more on multilateral economic cooperation such as WTO, and also trying to establish bilateral preferential trade relations through FTAs. The Korean government pursues diversification of trade and economic cooperation in international community while anticipating the improvement of trade environment by signing FTAs. At the same time, Korea is attempting to take advantage of FTAs to settle down its internal norms, to stabilize the

Korean Peninsula, and to achieve non-economic purposes. So far, Korea has signed FTAs with various countries including the US, EU, China, ASEAN, India, and others.

Even after joining the WTO, Russia signed various FTAs with the Commonwealth of Independent States (CIS). Russia has maintained its long-standing economic dependence with these countries while providing special trade benefits through the FTAs, as well as strengthening its political influence based on this point. Furthermore, Russia has recently signed strategic FTAs with countries that do not belong to the CIS members, including Vietnam, to pursue diverse trade relations, economic benefits, and non-economic objectives. (Kim 2013, 12)

3. Challenges for the Legal Cooperation including the Korea-Russia FTA

The more Korea continues to put in efforts to expand efficient economic cooperation and market openness by signing FTAs with major global countries, the more essential it becomes to settle a stable legal foundation. Furthermore, in the recent international community, such legal bases usually start from signing FTAs; Korea has signed numerous FTAs to expand trade and economic cooperation with various countries so far. As Russia also moves forward from emphasizing only the economic ties with the CIS countries, the possibility of an FTA with Korea has increased. The two partners already started the official talk on the FTA relation mainly in the investment area.

However, even if these two sides have the will to sign for the FTA, it cannot be actualized right away; in order to conclude the treaty, various procedures such as investigation and negotiation are necessary. In particular, efforts are needed to build up the environment for the Korea-Russia FTA, while addressing various domestic and international legal challenges. To this end, there should be legal discussions on a different level, more than simply securing the possibility and necessity of cooperation between Korea and Russia, and a cautious consideration of the FTA itself.

The Eurasian Economic Union (EAEU), a customs union that has Belarus, Kazakhstan, and Kyrgyzstan, was founded in responds to EU which is more focused on the Western Europe. According to this economic community's agreement on the establishment, all the member states must be included in the treaty, so long as one of the member states is willing to sign any economic agreements, such as FTAs, with third countries. In the end, the 'Korea-Russia FTA' will be expanded to 'Korea-EAEU FTA' negotiations under the regulation. Korea has already experienced similar situation while pushing for the FTAs with EU and ASEAN. The question is whether the economic effectiveness of the FTA with EAEU members, not Russia, is sufficient to cover up the potential adverse effects.

Changes in domestic laws in response to the FTA are also critical. There were progresses made in the domestic law, as several FTAs were signed, and a legal basis was prepared for consistency of policy through the enactment of the Trade Procedure Act. Now, domestic legal actions and FTA regulations are required to reflect technical development or industrial structure changes related to the development of the Arctic Circle. It is also necessary to define the grounds and principles for resolving issues of damage and compensation in traditional term which might be caused by the Korea-Russia FTA.

It is desirable to specify the principle of general compensation and the decision-making procedure in the implementation regulations to carry on the FTA. This is because in each situation where the affected industry has been specifically revealed, it will be politically sensitive to legislate compensation, and it may be difficult to secure the equity and objectivity. Only when these laws secure the neutrality of compensation and support and ensure the predictability, we can reduce the unconditional opposition on openness for the vulnerable industries. It is also necessary to stipulate that compensation and assistance should be made within the scope of the WTO subsidy agreement, so that it does not escalate into any trade dispute. Such details are also noted in special laws such as the FTA Special Act on Support for Farming and Fishing and the Trade Adjustment Assistance

Act.

The FTA can also contribute on the security issues regarding the Korean peninsula. Inter-Korean economic exchanges have a specialty which is somewhat different from transactions with other countries or within the domestic. Article 26 paragraph 1 of the Act on Inter-Korean Exchange and Cooperation states, "When it comes to trade, which is not specifically stipulated in this Act, it shall be governed by the Foreign Trade Act as provided under the Presidential Decree." In paragraph 4, it notes "In compliance with other laws under the provisions of paragraphs 1 to 3, special cases may be set against them under the Presidential Decree." In this sense, for the Korea-Russia FTA, it is suggested thar the specialty of the inter-Korea exchange, which implies that Korea and Russia's cooperation can have impact on peace for the Korean Peninsula.

Furthermore, it is also necessary for Korea to come up with a legal mechanism to recognize the granting preferential treatment through the FTA, considering its exchanges with the North as a special transaction within the nation – which is an exception to the principle of Most-Favored-Nation treatment in the WTO system. To this end, a special regional trade agreement can also be sought between the two Koreas on the basis of Article 9 paragraph 3 of WTO Agreement on Establishment. However, North Korea's entry into WTO must be managed beforehand in order to conclude a trade agreement between the two Koreas and obtain approval within the WTO rules. Since it is difficult to expect North Korea to sign for WTO at present, it is required to enact declarations through domestic laws, including the Act on Inter-Korean Exchange and Cooperation regarding the special relations between the two Koreas. (Kim 2018, 179-182)

Recently, North Korea has been making moves to be considered as 'a country of legal-conformity' in the international community despite the international economic sanctions. For example, North Korea is trying to be incorporated into the international trade environment and trade rules in a long-term perspective, including joining the CISG, which is a general treaty on international trade. Given that these images were hard to expect in the past, North Korea's such effort is certainly meaningful that it is preparing to facilitate economic exchanges within the entire Korean Peninsula in a long-term perspective. This is what needs to be considered in the process of signing the Korea-Russia FTA.

IV. Conclusion

Korea and Russia have expanded various areas of economic cooperation since they established diplomatic ties in the 1990s. Investment and commodity trade between the two have grown significantly, that seeing Korean products in the Russian market became a more common daily thing. Now that the two countries are looking for a new model of cooperation, to achieve further development of Russian Arctic Circle, the source of new marketability. Both Korea and Russia will be able to share the goals of regional development and transportation efficiency and create new markets through the development of the area.

As seen above, the two countries are already actualizing cooperation in broad spectrum for the region. With the rapid exploitation of resources due to climate change and technological development, Korean companies have begun to bring the real economic benefits, having positive effects on related industries such as the construction of transport and special ships. However, since there are some according troublesome aspects, measures that can lead to sustainable development through the supplementation of relevant norms are critical. Russia is also aware of these problems in obtaining economic benefits in the future; cooperation between the two countries should be extended to sufficiently cover this point.

The provisions of international law related to the Arctic Circle are vague and does not encompass every area. In addition, when it comes to the national interests, many situations rise from areas where international and national laws are not clearly harmonized. This is why international community's cooperation is essential; for example, there is a possibility of conflict between the international law regarding the Arctic shipping and domestic law of Russia. Therefore, efforts should be made to reflect the interests of both sides and to maintain economic benefits, in case Korea participates in Russia's development of the area, as well as for the legal foundation to reduce negative issues.

There are many ways for realizing what are mentioned aforehand, but we can specifically propose a Korea-Russia FTA. In the process of pursuing it, the government should also consider various tasks, such as harmonizing with the FTAs Korea has been signing, and dealing with the domestic law in accordance with the new FTA, based on the previous experiences. From Russia's point of view, special circumstances such as the EAEU should be taken in consideration. The two countries also have to conduct preemptive research on the efficient use of the FTA, which is the legal basis.

The process of signing the FTA, which will serve as the international legal basis for cooperation between the partners, should be clearly marked for the purpose of 'Sustainable Arctic Development.' Furthermore, these propositions should be able to be digested in the process of utilizing FTAs and readjusting domestic and international regulations, as well as the joint respond to the emergence of new industries, markets, and even unforeseen issues. In Korea's perspective, it should consider the possibility that the FTA could be used in non-economic areas such as on the Korean Peninsula issue.

Reference

Baker, James. "Maersk considers northern sea route service," *Lloyd's List*, (14 July 2019).

Hodges, Jeremy Shiryaevskaya, Anna & Khrennikova, Dina. "Melting Ice in the Arctic Is Opening a New Energy Trade Route," *Bloomberg* (28 August 2018).

Humpert, Malte & Raspotnik, Andreas. "The Future of Arctic Shipping Along the Transpolar Sea Route," *Arctic Yearbook 2012*, (2012).

Jeh, Sung-Hoon & Min, Ji-Young. "Russian Arctic Development Strategy and New Possibility for Korea-Russia Cooperation," *KIEP World Economy Update*, Vol. 4 No. 20 (2014).

Kim, Bongchul. "Regional Trade Agreements of Korea and Russia-The Possibility of the Korea-Russia FTA," *The Korean Journal of Slavic Studies*, Vol. 29 No. 1 (2013).

Kim, Bongchul. "The changes of Korean Domestic Laws with the FTA system," *Chonbuk Law Review*, No. 44 (2015).

Kim, Bongchul. "The Evolution of Korean FTAs and Rediscovery of the Legal Function," *The International Commerce & Law Review*, No. 79 (2018).

Kim, Sang-Won. "Western Economic Sanctions and Russian Arctic Development: Focusing on Natural Gas," *Slav newspaper*, Vol. 32 No. 4 (2017).

Rho, Young-don & Park, Won. "An Analysis of the Russia's Bill of the Federal Law on the Water Areas of Northern Sea Route," *Seoul International Law Journal*, Vol. 18 No. 2 (2011).

Park, Jong-Kwan. "Russian Transport Logistics Development Strategy: Focusing on the 'Arctic Region'," *Slav newspaper*, Vol. 30 No. 1 (2016).

Park, Jin-Hee & Lee, Min-Gyu. "A Study on Competitiveness and Effect Analysis for Developing a Port Specialized in Northern Sea Route ," *Journal of Navigation and Port Research*, Vol. 39 No. 3 (2015).

Seidler, Christoph. *Arktisches Monopoly: Der Kampf um die Rohstoffe der Polarregion*, (translated by Mihwa Park, Seoul: The soup, 2010).

Staalesen, Atle. "Russia's Far East Ministry to Get Powers over Arctic policy." *The Independent Barents Observer* (21 January, 2019).

Yun, Yeong-Mi. "Strategy of Russian Marine Security over the North Pole Region: Focusing on the development of the Arctic Ocean and the Marine Cooperation between Korea and Russia on the North Pole," *East and West Studies*, Vol. 21 No. 2 (2009).

Zadorin, Maksim Klisheva, Olga Vezhlivtseva, Ksenia & Antufieva, Daria. *Russian Laws on Indigenous Issues. Guarantees, Communities, Territories of Traditional Land Use: Translated and Commented* (Rovaniemi: University of Lapland, 2017).

Demographic characteristics of the Arctic Region in Russia:

Population and Migration Trend Analysis

Wooik Choi

I. Introduction

Global warming is becoming more prominent in the late 20th and early 21st centuries. As the temperature in the Arctic rises, various ideas and plans on commercializing the Arctic routes and developing the Arctic industries are taking shape. In addition, changes in the climate and natural environment due to rising temperatures are affecting not only the industrial development but also the space of life surrounding humans. Thus, multiple followings of social changes are occurring in cities and other local areas in the Arctic region. This study, particularly, focuses on the analysis of demographic characteristics, such as population and migration trends in Russian Arctic region.

Residents of Russian Arctic area are either ethnic minorities who have lived here for hundreds or thousands of years or Russians who recently moved to here. These Russians came for labor, operations, and management for the development and preservation of the region, despite the severe cold and poor living conditions. The ethnic minorities, who had long lived and preserved their life styles in the Arctic, experienced a huge social upheaval due to Russia's socialist modernization in the early 20th century. However, with the collapse of 70 year-long socialist system, the market reforms began at the end of the 20th century. Then people in the Arctic happened to experience social and economic turbulence again. Moreover, recent developments in the Arctic industry have accelerated the changes within the region.

Under these circumstances, determining in which social and economic conditions the people of Russian Arctic are placed is critical data to predict their further lives. In addition, in order to constantly develop the industries in Arctic without difficulty, they need to play the role of development and preservation as the main actors. Therefore, research in where they are standing now and where they will be must be a significant task.

From the end of the 20th century to the early 21st century, research on the Arctic began in earnest. However, in fact, the researches were mainly in the field of natural science, international relations and foreign policies, or industrial and economic aspects surrounding the Arctic interests. Research in the field of humanities and social society just recently began with the recognition of importance. For example, studies on the survival of the Arctic minorities and their culture preservation, as well as the health and environmental pollution of residents. However, only few studies of demographic characteristics of all the Arctic residents, including minorities, have been done properly. Of course, the problem of decrease or outflow of population has been pointed out in some areas, but these issues have often been addressed mainly as the research results obtained incidentally through other studies.

Here are some examples of representative studies:
Health Transition in Arctic Population, published in 2007 by T. Kue Young and Peter Bjerregaard, introduces the situation in the Arctic to the world. It covers ethnic minorities who are currently living there, their environment, and diseases. In this study, the population problem at this moment is not addressed in depth. It is simply mentioning that the population is rapidly decreasing in Russian Arctic region between 1989 and 2000, and that the outflow of non-native populations was cited as particularly severe. (Young & Bjerregaard 2007, 90-91)

Professor Han Jong-man, who leads the domestic Arctic research, deals with comprehensive analysis of Russian Arctic geography, humanities, and political economy in his book "Understanding the Russian Arctic," published in 2010. However, when it comes to population issues, it is briefly introducing ethnic minorities, languages, and urban information. (Han et al. 2010) In "Демографические процессы, динамика трудовых ресурсов и риски здоровью населения европейской части Арктической зоныРоссии" published in 2016 by Б. А. Ревичи, it attempts to seriously go into demographic study in Russian Arctic. A wide range of topics, including demographic processes, ethnic minorities, health, environmental issues, and labor resources, have been studied. However, still there was limitation to the Arctic region of Europe-Russia (Western Russia from the Ural Mountains). (Ревичи и др. 2016) Although humanities and social science studies of the Russian Arctic have been recently conducted and have produced quality research results, the demographic studies of the Arctic population are still at a rudimentary stage. (Choi 2018)

This study aims to analyze demographic characteristics throughout Russian Arctic area based on demographic data accumulated for nearly 30 years since the market reform period. Nevertheless, as will be delivered in chapter II, the data of demographic and regional information from Russia's National Statistical Office are scattered in various resources. In addition, within the same data published each year, statistical data are partially provided in respective periods. Therefore, the purpose of this study is to systematically organize and analyze demographic characteristics, trends, and flows in the Russian Arctic region by compiling and reconstructing these statistical data. This work is done by comparing the human sphere and migration trends between the entire population of Russia and the Arctic, and by comparing the Arctic regions one to the other.

Following the introduction of Chapter I, this paper expounds the definition of the Russian Arctic and the data of the Russia's National Statistical Office in Chapter II, and the population trend of the Russian Arctic in Chapter III, migration trend in Chapter IV. Finally, Chapter V will summarize and the research results.

II. Definition of the Russian Arctic and Russia's National Statistical Office's data

From the late 2000s, the Russian government began to establish policies related to the Arctic development and carried out various projects. In fact, as Russia has the world's largest Arctic ocean and territory, the North Pole is inevitably a new frontier for its national development. In September 2008, the Russian government approved the 'Basic Russian Federal Policy on Arctic by 2020 and thereafter.' This policy calls for 1) expanding the resources base of the Arctic region to meet domestic demand for hydrocarbon and marine biological resources, 2) preserving the Arctic ecosystem, 3) preventing environmental damage followed by increasing economic activity and climate change, and 4) promoting the development of information and communication, science and technology, and international cooperation in the Arctic region. (Jeh & Min 2013, 50)

In 2013, Putin approved the 'Russian Federation's Arctic

Development and National Security Strategy by 2020.' This accordingly is consisted of various projects including 1) development of chrome, manganese, tin, aluminum, uranium, titanium, and zinc fields in the Arctic, and 2) development of the eastern Arctic region of the Ural Mountains, and the Timan-Pechora oil and gas basins, as well as the hydrocarbon fields in Barents Sea, Pechora Sea, Kara Sea, and Yamal Peninsula, Gydan Peninsula continental shelfs. (Jeh & Min 2013, 64) In addition, other projects to develop the Arctic shipping routes have been actively underway since the 2010s, with port facilities being modernized in central Igarka, Dudinka, Dixon, Tiksi, Pevek, and Provideniya, and new transport vessels are being built. (Макар 2015, 85-96)

Korea is also showing interest in Russia's Arctic route and Arctic development projects in line with the New Northern Policy. Korea's Daewoo Shipbuilding & Marine Engineering has received orders to build an icebreaking LNG carrier in connection with Russia's Yamal project and so on. As such, development of Arctic has been brisk in Russia from the 2000s to the 2010s. Therefore, we can fully assume that the lives of Russian residents in the Arctic region are also undergoing a major change.

This study focuses on the analysis of the demographic characteristics of the Russian Arctic region, which stands at the center of the change. First of all, it is necessary to define the boundaries of Russian Arctic area as the subject of study. According to the Russian Federal Act of 2013, the Russian Presidential Decree of March 2014, and the Additional Presidential Decree of June 2017, the Russian Arctic region is as shown in <Table 1>.

<Table 1> Russian Arctic Region

	Russian Arctic Region	Note
1	Murmansk Region	The entire territory
2	Nenets Autonomous Area	The entire territory
3	Chukotka Autonomous Area	The entire territory
4	Yamal-Nenets Autonomous Area	The entire territory
5	Komi Republic	1 City (Воркута)
6	Republic of Sakha	5 Districts (Аллаиховский, Анабарский национальный, Булунский, Нижнеколымский, Усть-Янский)
7	Krasnoyarsk Territory	1 City (Норильск) 2 Districts (Таймырский Долгано-Ненецкий, Туруханский)
8	Arkhangelsk Region	3 Cities (Архангельск, Новодвинск, Северодвинск) 3 Districts (М езенский, Онежский, Приморский) Island (Новая Земля)
9	The Arctic Ocean and islands	-
10	Republic of Karelia (Added in 2017)	3 Districts (Беломорский, Лоухский, Кемский)

Source: Arctic Megapedia. Арктическая зона Российской Федерации. http://arctic- megapedia.ru/wiki/Арктическая_зона_Российской_Федерации (retrieved on 2018.03.02.) / Политобразование. Арктическая зона Российской Федерации(АЗРФ). http://lawinrussia.ru/content/arkticheskaya-zona-rossiyskoy-federacii-azrf(retrieved on 2018.03.17.).

Four of these areas, Murmansk, Nenets, Chukotka, and Yamal-Nenets, are where the entire territory of the province (autonomous region) falls into the Arctic region. According to Russian legislation, five other regions, excluding the ninth 'the Arctic Ocean and islands,' only partial northern areas of the territory are included in the Arctic. In fact, there is no absolute standard for setting boundaries in the Arctic. For example, according to natural science standards, the Arctic is 1) where the isothermal line is below 10 degrees in July, 2) beyond the northern boundary of the forest distribution zone, and 3) areas above 66.33 degrees' north latitude. However, in countries with Arctic territory, the boundaries of the Arctic are not actually set by this natural science standard, but are likely divided by the administrative boundaries of the region. It is also possible to define the Arctic within the humanities or social science terms, where historical, cultural, geopolitical, socio-economical aspects of the area are considered. <Figure 1> shows the range of the Russian Arctic according to this criterion. The dark colored zone of <Figure 1> is the North Pole, and the light colored zone is the areas considered as same as the North Pole.

<Figure 1> Russian Arctic: boundary according to humanities and social-science factors

Source: Районный крайнего севера России. https://yandex.ru/images/search?text=районный_крайнего_севера_россии (retrieved on 2018.03.02.) / Северный (Арктический) федеральный университет. Российская Арктика или Арктическая зона?. http://narfu.ru/aan/Encyclopedia_Arctic/RA-AZRF.PDF(retrieved on 2016.07.02.).

According to this standard, about 70% of Russia's entire territory is in the Arctic or the area where is equivalent to the Arctic. Therefore, most of the areas of No.5 to No.10 in <Table 1> are classified as the Arctic and its equivalent, as shown in <Figure 1>. In addition, according to 2009 data from Russia's National Statistical Office, areas No.1 to No.4 on <Table 1> are classified as the Arctic region as well as the whole area of Karelia, Komi, Sakha, Arkhangelsk are within the Arctic or equivalent area. Most cities and provinces in Krasnoyarsk are also classified as the Arctic or equivalent regions also (Федеральная служба государственной статистики). Therefore, by definition by humanities and social science standards, all states, autonomous regions, and republics presented under the Act in <Table 1> can be viewed as the Arctic regions. In other words, setting and analyzing all the listed areas in <Table 1> as the Arctic regions of Russia does not deviate from the purpose of this study; which is to analyze demographic characteristics rather than the natural science. Accordingly, in this study has 9 listed areas in <Table 1>, excluding the 'The Arctic Ocean and islands,' as the scope of study. Then, based on statistics of 9 areas, demographic characteristics will be analyzed.

The basic socio-economic indicators of the Russian Arctic region analyzed in this study are as follows. As of 2018, the total area of the Arctic region was about 8.27 million km2, accounting for about 48 percent of the entire Russia. However, there are only 7.8 million residents in the Arctic which is about 5.3% of Russia's total population, and 3.95 million people are employed, which is only 5.5% of the total number of people employed in Russia. The number of population and employed are much smaller, considering the size of the Arctic region, as most of these areas are frontier regions and hard for residents to live due to the harsh climate and conditions.

Meanwhile, Russian Arctic region's gross domestic product is estimated at 6.5561 trillion rubles as of 2018, which accounts for about 9.5% of Russia's total, indicating that the region has a fairly large proportion of economy compared to its population (Росстат

2018, 18-23). Although circumstances depend on economic conditions, Karelia (18%), Arkhangelsk (22%), and Krasnoyarsk (32%) have the largest share of manufacturing in the region, while many other regions, such as Komi (35%), Nenets (75%), Murmansk (16%), Yamal-Nenets (55%), Sakha (52%), and Chukotka (50%), have the largest share of the most useful minerals in the region. In Karelia and Krasnoyarsk, the Arctic region is generally seen as the most advanced mining area for underground resources, because their mineral mining proportion follows its manufacturing (12% and 19%, respectively). (Росстат 2018, 478-479)

The analysis of this study is based on data from the Russia's National Statistical Office. Russia's National Statistical Office publishes various data related to demographic indicators. However, statistical indicators for the Arctic region require 85 federal entities, in other words, regional statistical information. That's because it is the only way to get statistical information on nine Russian Arctic regions. These regional demographic indices are derived from the following limited data from Russia's National Statistical Office.

- *Russian region: Social-Economic Indicator (Регионы России. Социально-экономические показатели)*
- *Regional information in Russian Population Yearbook (Демографический ежегодник России)*
- *Regional information in Russian Labor and Employment (Труд и занятость в России)*

- *Regional information in Russian Statistical Yearbook (Российский статический ежегодник)*

This study analyzes 30-year data from the early 1990s when market reforms began to take place. Currently, "Regions in Russia: Social-Economic Indicators" has been published in 2018, while "Russian Population Yearbook" and "Russian Labor and Employment" have yet to be published till the 2017 edition. However, each data is compiled with statistical information for the year before its publication. Therefore, the study period for this paper will be from the early 1990s to 2016 or 2017. Each statistic is published annually or biennially.

Because this study particularly focuses on trends in population and migration, it is necessary to aggregate the statistical indicators provided annually into a single table. Each table will provide a footnote in the publication year of the data, or, if necessary, a description of how certain statistical indicators have been aggregated and reconstructed will be narrated in the body. And there are some statistics that has been provided for only a few years at a given time. If this is also necessary, a related explanation will be added in the text or footnote.

Therefore, in this study, we're focusing on the significant demographic statistics, such as population and migration. The analysis on demographic characteristics and types of the Russian Arctic region will be held by tracking the pattern and change of time series flows from the 1990s to the 2000s and until recently in the 2010s. To this end, this study mainly reconstructs and analyzes statistical information and indicators of various data published by the Russia's National Statistical Office. In addition, the research results of various academic and research institutes were utilized as reference materials.

III. Population Trends in the Russian Arctic

The population of a country is basically determined by the natural increase and decrease of its population and by the migration, in other words, the influx and outflow of its population. Chapter III deals with populations in the Russian Arctic and Chapter IV with migration of populations. <Table 2> summarizes the flows in the population of Russia and the Arctic on a five-year basis from 1990 to present, using Russia's National Statistical Office data "Russia Region: Social-Economic Indicators." Russia's total population was about 148 million in the early 1990s. Then began to decrease rapidly and by the late 2000s it had reached to about 142 million. It then increased again in the 2010s to about 147 million by 2017.

<Table 2> The flows in the population of Russia and the Arctic (Unit: 1,000)

	1990	1995	2000	2005	2010	2015	2017
Russia	148,274	148,292	146,304	143,236	142,865	146,545	146,880
Karelia	791	764	729	676	643	630	622
Komi	1,240	1,133	1,043	963	899	857	841
Arkhangelsk	1,517	1,433	1,328	1,240	1,183	1,130	1,111
Nenets	52	43	41	42	42	44	44
Murmansk	1,189	1,037	923	839	794	762	754
Yamal	489	487	498	517	525	534	538
Krasnoyarsk	3,163	3,100	3,001	2,869	2,829	2,866	2,876
Sakha	1,119	1,020	958	954	958	960	964
Chukotka	158	84	57	52	51	50	50
Total	9,718	9,101	8,578	8,152	7,924	7,833	7,800

Source: Росстат, 2018: 39-40, 2010b: 56-57.

<Table 3> Natural increase rate of population of Russia and the Arctic

(Unit: number of every 1,000)

	90	95	00	05	06	07	08	09	10	11	12	13	14	15	16	17
Russia	2.2	-5.7	-6.6	-5.9	-4.8	-3.3	-2.5	-1.8	-1.7	-0.9	-0.0	0.2	0.2	0.3	-0.0	-0.9
Karelia	3.1	-7.9	-7.8	-8.2	-6.8	-5.3	-5.1	-4.0	-4.1	-2.8	-2.8	-2.7	-2.3	-3.1	-2.8	-4.3
Komi	6.1	-3.5	-3.5	-4.1	-2.7	-0.8	-0.5	-0.4	-0.2	0.7	1.8	2.2	2.0	1.3	0.7	-0.3
Arkhangelsk	3.7	-6.1	-7.5	-6.3	-4.9	-2.8	-2.6	-2.1	-2.3	-1.9	-1.2	-0.7	-0.9	-1.4	-1.9	-2.7
Nenets	10.3	0.7	0.3	2.3	1.1	3.0	3.6	4.8	4.7	4.7	7.1	5.7	7.9	8.4	9.6	6.6
Murmansk	5.4	-3.2	-3.0	-3.6	-2.9	-1.4	-1.3	-1.2	-0.2	0.0	0.5	0.9	0.3	0.3	-0.3	-0.8
Yamal	13.1	6.7	6.1	7.7	7.6	8.8	9.1	9.7	10.3	10.2	11.4	11.5	11.8	11.3	10.1	9.1
Krasnoyarsk	4.5	-4.2	-5.5	-4.9	-2.9	-1.5	-0.7	0.2	0.1	0.5	1.5	1.7	1.7	1.7	1.4	0.1
Sakha	12.7	5.5	4.0	4.1	4.7	6.4	6.1	7.0	7.0	7.7	8.5	8.8	9.2	8.6	7.6	6.4
Chukotka	10.1	1.3	1.9	3.9	3.7	4.1	2.7	1.2	0.9	2.5	2.6	2.6	2.8	4.1	3.6	3.7
Total	69.0	-10.7	-15	-9.1	-3.1	10.5	11.3	15.2	16.2	21.6	29.4	30.0	32.5	31.2	28.0	17.8

Source: 1990-2010, the data were reconstructed from: Росстат, 2011: 68-69. 2011-2017, the data were reconstructed from: Росстат, 2018: 71-72. Arkhangelsk's pre-2010 figure includes Nenets, and from 2010, Arkhangelsk and Nenets are calculated respectively.

However, in 2017, the population of the Arctic region has declined by 1.92 million (20%) from about 9.72 million in 1990 to 7.8 million, and the decline continues to present. Among these, however, Yamal-Nenets exceptionally had a small increase after decline shortly in the early 1990s. In addition, in the case of Nenets, Krasnoyarsk, and Sakha, the population is growing gradually, albeit slightly, in the recent 2010s. However, in many areas other than this, the population continued to decrease over the entire period. Thus, the demographic situation in the Arctic region can generally be assessed as negative.

The major factors affecting the increase and decrease of the population are the natural increase (or decrease) and inflow (or outflow). First of all, Chapter III deals with natural increases and decreases in population. <Table 3> uses the data from Russia's National Statistical Office "Russian Region: Social-Economic Indicators" to summarize the natural flow of the population in the Russian Arctic from 1990 until recently.

According to <Table 3>, Russia as a whole began to experience negative natural growth, in other words, the natural decrease in the early 1990s, when 2000 was the year when the natural decrease rate was the highest at -6.6. However, the natural growth of the population began since 2013. Across the Arctic region, natural population decreased continued until 2006, but natural increase began in 2007. Thus, considering the Russian population as a whole began to naturally increase since 2013, the Arctic region already was going through it since 2007. Still, the reason that the entire population decline in the Arctic region continues to this day is because the outflow of people goes on in a larger scale. This population outflow is discussed in chapter IV.

As observed, both the Russian and the entire Arctic Region had natural increase of population around 2010. However, despite the beginning of the natural increase, the past natural decline in the population has left quite a serious aftereffect. This is illustrated by the age distribution trend of the Russia population. Among Russia's total population, the youth population ratio was 24.3% in 1990, which fell rapidly to 16.0% in 2007 and then slightly recovered to 18.6% in 2017. The proportion of youth population has fallen so rapidly, because the demographic situation has worsened due to the transitional situation in the market reform period. For example, the infant mortality rate soared, the marriage rate dropped, and the divorce rate rose which lowered the birth rate. Furthermore, the historical background of 20th century also contributed a part. (Choi, 2011) Meanwhile, the percentage of the elderly population was 19% in 1990, then steadily grew to 20.4% in 2000, 20.5% in 2005, 22.3% in 2010, and 25.4% in 2017. (Росстат 2012b, 64-69; 2018, 47-52) The proportion of youth population among Russia's total population gradually rises in the late 2000s, and in all regions of the Arctic, this rate has increased since the mid-2000s. The percentage of the elderly population has also been on the rise since the mid-2000s, both in

Russia's entire population or in Russia's Arctic region. What matters is how the working population rate is changing.

<Table 4> Trends in the proportion of working population in Russia and the Arctic (Unit: %)

	90	00	05	06	07	08	09	10	11	12	13	14	15	16	17
Russia	56.7	60.2	63.0	63.0	62.9	62.6	62.0	61.5	60.9	60.1	59.3	58.4	57.4	56.7	56.0
Karelia	57.8	61.8	64.3	64.1	63.5	62.9	62.0	61.1	60.1	59.2	58.2	57.2	56.1	55.2	54.5
Komi	61.6	64.9	67.5	67.3	66.9	66.4	65.4	64.5	63.5	62.4	61.3	60.2	59.0	58.0	57.1
Arkhangelsk	57.7	61.9	64.4	64.3	63.9	63.3	62.3	61.3	60.3	59.2	58.2	57.2	56.1	55.2	54.5
Nenets	61.1	62.9	65.8	65.9	65.6	64.8	63.7	62.9	62.1	61.2	60.5	59.6	58.6	57.6	56.8
Murmansk	64.5	67.9	68.6	68.3	67.6	67.0	66.1	65.3	64.4	63.6	62.5	61.6	60.6	59.7	59.1
Yamal	65.3	69.9	72.6	72.7	72.2	71.6	70.7	70.1	70.1	69.6	68.6	67.6	66.2	65.1	64.3
Krasnoyarsk	58.9	62.3	64.9	64.9	64.7	64.3	63.6	63.0	62.3	61.5	60.6	59.7	58.7	58.0	57.2
Sakha	60.8	62.6	65.3	65.5	65.3	65.1	64.4	63.9	63.1	62.3	61.4	60.5	59.5	58.8	58.1
Chukotka	67.7	69.5	71.5	71.0	70.3	69.2	68.0	67.1	67.0	66.5	65.8	64.9	64.0	63.2	62.3
Average	61.7	64.9	67.2	67.11	66.7	66.1	65.1	64.4	63.7	62.8	61.9	60.9	59.9	59.0	58.2

Source: Росстат, 2012: 64-69, 2018: 47-52. Arkhangelsk's pre-2010 figure includes Nenets, and from 2010, Arkhangelsk and Nenets are calculated respectively.

<Table 4> summarizes the trends in the proportion of working population in the Arctic from the 1990s to the present, using the Russian National Statistical Office data, "Russian Region: Social-Economic Indicators." According to this report, the working population of Russia's total population in 1990 was 56.7%, which gradually increased to 63% in 2005 and 2006. However, the ratio has since fallen rapidly to 56% in 2017, just over a decade. Despite the demographic situation of the transitional market reform period, the

percentage of the working population increased from 1990 to the mid-2000s, because the ones who born in 1970s and 1980s turned into the working age group in 1990s. In the 1970s and 1980s, birth rate was stably maintained, therefore, the proportion of youth population increased every year during this period. (Росстат 2001a, 40) In the 1990s, however, the worsening demographic situation reduced the size of the births, and as they entered the working age group from the mid-2000s, the proportion of the working population was lowered in earnest.

Of course, the natural population growth began to appear in Russia in 2007, however, the percentage of youth population increased only 2.6% from 16.0% in 2007 to 18.6% in 2017. Furthermore, the elderly population increased by 4.3% from 21.1% in 2007 to 25.4% in 2017, which is larger than the inflow of the working population. (Росстат 2012b, 64-69; 2018, 47-52) In order for the natural population growth after 2000s to be led to an increase in the working population, it might need more than 15 years, which is after 2030. Similar to the pattern of the whole in Russian population, the employment proportion of the population in the Arctic region has increased until the mid-2000s, but has gradually decreased ever since. However, while Russia's proportion of working population dropped by 7% from 63.0% in 2005 to 56.0% in 2017, the Arctic went through a bigger gap of 9% from 67.2% to 58.2%, indicating that the proportion of working population in the Arctic region went way lower. Especially, the proportion of the working population in Karelia and Arkhangelsk began to fall even lower than Russia's overall average since 2010. However, the average rate of working population in the Arctic region was always higher than the average proportion of Russia's total population. It is 5% higher in 1990, 4% higher in the mid-2000s, and 2.2% higher in 2017. The ratio of Yamal-Nenets and Chukotka is about 6 to 8% higher as of 2017. This can be attributed to the fact that the Arctic region is not suitable for long-term residence for a family in a harsh climate natural environment. It rather has more temporary working population or relatively young people who stay for only a short period for labor compared to other areas. However, it can be assessed that the demographic situation caused by the labor shortage in Russia's Arctic region is quite serious, given that the average rate of the working population in the Arctic is now falling faster than the average of the entire Russia, and that some areas are already lower than it.

IV. Migration Trends in the Russian Arctic

The quantitative proportion of the working population in the Russian Arctic is declining, but the natural growth of the population has already begun in the mid-2000s. However, so far, Russia's Arctic population is declining overall. That is because, as shown below, the outflow of people continues on a scale which goes beyond the growth.

<Table 5> Fluctuation of Migration in Russia's Arctic Region

(Unit: per 10,000)

	90	95	00	05	06	07	08	09	10	11	12	13	14	15	16	17
Russia	19	44	25	20	22	25	25	24	19	22	21	21	19	17	18	14
Karelia	-35	-16	-13	-115	-93	-29	-33	-36	-54	-18	-15	-13	-7	-12	-16	-31
Komi	-134	-176	-108	-163	-162	-98	-129	-109	-139	-112	-122	-120	-107	-102	-81	-112
Arkhangelsk	-78	-88	-78	-72	-70	-46	-61	-49	-83	-81	-88	-85	-68	-72	-56	-70
Nenets	-169	-271	-62	-21	-26	-19	-47	14	-50	32	12	-3	1	23	-73	-53
Murmansk	-77	-250	-165	-169	-156	-93	-105	-60	-69	-77	-101	-129	-65	-57	-57	-46
Yamal	-143	120	-22	-24	4	-45	-114	-79	-88	118	-21	-150	-112	-223	-65	-45
Krasnoyarsk	-27	-5	-16	-64	-54	-15	-8	-1	-15	28	13	5	3	10	17	3
Sakha	-60	-219	-92	-28	-29	-34	-69	-66	-71	-102	-87	-96	-70	-56	-43	-48
Chukotka	-355	-1,269	-704	73	64	-56	-156	-196	-174	102	-66	-70	-30	-117	-103	-132
Average	-120	-242	-140	-65	-58	-48	-80	-65	-83	-12	-53	-73	-51	-67	-53	-59

Source: The following data of 1990–2000 were reconstructed from: Росстат, 2011: 76-77. 2005-2012 were also reconstructed from: Росстат, 2013b: 79-80, 2013-2017 from. Росстат, 2018: 87-88. The previous figure for Arkhangelsk in 2010 was calculated by including Nenets, and from the 2010 figure, Arkhangelsk and Nenets went separately.

<Table 5> summarizes the trend of migration flow of the population in Russian Arctic region from the 1990s to the present, using the Russia's National Statistical Office data "Russian Region: Social-Economic Indicators." The table shows the annual net outflow and net inflow, with adjustment of inflow and outflow of the population. This shows that since the 1990s, the outflow volume is larger than the inflow, which makes the net outflow continued in most of the Arctic regions. The Arctic region in the 1990s and early 2000s, the average net outflow was over 100 per 10,000 people, and the

average net outflow from the mid-2000s to 2017 reached 50 to 80 per 10,000 people each year. Only in the case of Krasnoyarsk, the net inflow began to occur on a very small scale from 2011 to 2017. In addition, Nenets also had a small net inflow in the 2010s only four years. The outflow of the population from Russia's Arctic region has been attributed, among other things, to the collapse of various support systems and social infrastructure which was responsible by the government during the Soviet era. The survival in the region has basically became individuals' full responsibility. (Силин 2016, 33-41)

However, it is not just the outflow of population, but the inflow is as brisk as the outflow in the Arctic region. The 2015 and 2016 "Russian Statistical Yearbook" provide the inflow and outflow of population by respective federal entity from 2012 to 2015. The figures are compiled in <Table 6>. <Table 6> shows that most of the Arctic regions have higher rates of inflow and outflow than the Russian average. Between 2012 and 2015, Russia's entire population has an annual inflow and outflow ratio of around 3%. In Russia's Arctic region, however, only Arkhangelsk's inflow ratio between 2012 and 2015 was slightly lower or equal to that of the entire Russia population, and all the other regions and all periods exceed the rate of migration in Russia's entire population. In particular, Nenets, Murmansk, Yamal-Nenets, and Chukotka have two to three times higher rates of migration than Russia's entire population, whether it is inflow or outflow. In particular, Murmansk, Yamal-Nenets, and Chukotka have higher rates of out-of-area migration than within the region. 2017 as an example, Murmansk and Yamal-Nenets account for about 2/3, while Chukotka account for about 4/5 of the out-of-area migration. (Росстат 2018, 89-100) What <Table 6> shows is that most of all, Russian Arctic regions are having actively moving population, regardless it is inflow or outflow.

This is basically possible, because job markets are expanded due to the development of the Russian Arctic industry, resulting an active labor input from the outside world. However, it is not so easy to live in these areas for a long time, because of natural and social environment constraints, therefore, there are many cases that people leave after working for a short period of time, so the ratio of inflow and outflow of the population is higher than those from other regions. Despite both the inflow and outflow are larger than other regions, as the outflow volume is larger, the migration from Russian Arctic to the outer world is continued for quite a long time. However, for international residents, migration toward Russian Arctic region is steadily maintained.

Russia's National Statistical Office shows the status of net inflow and net outflow of international residents by respective federal states(regional) in Russia, since 2004. <Table 7> shows the collected data from "Russian Population Yearbook" of every year.

<Table 6>

Fluctuation of Migration by Federations in Russia's Arctic Region

	2012	2013	2014	2015	2012	2013	2014	2015	2012	2013	2014	2015
	Inflow (Unit: Person)				**Outflow** (Unit: Person)				**Net inflow** (Unit: Person)			
	Inflow (Unit: %)				**Outflow** (Unit: %)				**Net inflow** (Unit: %)			
Russia	4,196,143	4,496,861	4,663,427	4,734,523	3,901,213	4,201,002	4,363,437	4,489,139	294,930	295,859	299,990	245,384
	2.9	3.1	3.2	3.2	2.7	2.9	3.0	3.1	0.2	0.2	0.2	0.2
Karelia	19,173	22,017	23,262	23,668	20,145	22,815	23,702	24,402	-972	-798	-440	-734
	3.0	3.5	3.6	3.8	3.1	3.6	3.8	3.8	-0.2	-0.1	-0.1	-0.1
Komi	28,770	29,876	32,931	32,931	39,556	40,410	42,234	41,669	-10,786	-10,534	-9,303	-8,738
	3.3	3.4	3.8	3.9	4.5	4.6	4.8	4.9	-1.2	-1.2	-1.1	-1.0
Arkhangelsk	33,917	35,086	34,316	36,257	44,211	44,922	42,043	44,376	-10,294	-9,836	-7,727	-8,119
	2.9	3.0	3.0	3.2	3.8	3.9	3.7	3.9	-0.9	-0.9	-0.7	-0.7
Nenets	2,380	2,549	2,217	2,167	2,330	2,561	2,211	2,066	50	-12	6	101
	5.5	5.9	5.2	4.9	5.4	6.0	5.1	4.7	0.1	-0.0	0.0	0.2
Murmansk	33,381	33,582	37,933	38,186	41,306	43,599	42,931	42,570	-7,925	-10,017	-4,998	-4,384
	4.3	4.4	5.0	5.0	5.3	5.7	5.6	5.6	-1.0	-1.3	-0.7	-0.6
Yamal	44,217	44,191	43,252	35,835	45,344	52,315	49,320	47,807	-1,127	-8,124	-6,068	-11,972
	8.2	8.2	8.0	6.7	8.4	9.7	9.1	9.0	-0.2	-1.5	-1.1	-2.2
Krasnoyarsk	102,529	110,347	113,508	117,098	98,736	108,956	112,573	114,345	3,793	1,391	935	2,753
	3.6	3.9	4.0	4.1	3.5	3.8	3.9	4.0	0.1	0.0	0.0	0.1
Sakha	33,005	33,042	31,486	36,456	41,364	42,172	38,194	41,843	-8,359	-9,130	-6,708	-5,387
	3.5	3.5	3.3	3.8	4.3	4.4	4.0	4.4	-0.9	-1.0	-0.7	-0.6
Chukotka	3,955	4,673	4,814	4,392	4,291	5,027	4,968	4,981	-336	-354	-154	-589
	7.8	9.2	9.4	9.9	8.4	9.9	9.7	10.0	-0.7	-0.7	-0.3	-1.2

Source: Росстат, 2015c: 100-101, 2016b: 99-100.

<Table 7> Annual Net Inflow Trends of International Migrants in Russia's Arctic Region (Unit: person)

	2004	2005	2006	2007	2008	2009	2011	2012	2013	2014	2016
Russia	39,362	107,432	132,319	239,943	242,106	247,449	319,761	294,930	295,859	270,036	261,948
Karelia	-167	-44	56	965	730	623	756	1,029	1102	939	239
Komi	-741	-603	-133	1,207	347	355	1,314	701	970	320	686
Arkhangelsk	44	-19	47	1,050	820	539	622	292	167	582	979
Nenets	11	8	21	59	31	46	89	81	92	166	73
Murmansk	-49	-51	-150	428	539	1,423	2,161	1,221	1,061	1,698	806
Yamal	204	1,370	1,424	1,603	1,584	1,403	8,870	3,390	2,521	3,146	1,189
Krasnoyarsk	-1,256	574	1,371	5,509	6,036	6,717	6,563	5,253	6,117	5,203	7,634
Sakha	-78	145	293	611	772	582	684	926	489	284	657
Chukotka	-2	25	66	41	45	47	240	14	258	260	78
Total	-2,034	1,405	2,995	11,473	10,904	11,735	21,299	12,907	12,777	12,598	12,341
Percentage	-	1.3%	2.3%	4.8%	4.5%	4.7%	6.7%	4.4%	4.3%	4.7%	4.7%

Source: the data were reconstructed from: Росстат, 2005: 532-537, 2006: 484-489, 2007: 470-475, 2008: 472-477, 2009: 477-482, 2010: 458-463, 2012: 468-473, 2013: Annex 7-9, 2014: Annex 7-7, 2015: Annex 7-7, 2017: Annex 7-7. No data on 2010, 2015, 2017 because of the no publish of Росстат in 2011, 2016 and 2018.

According to <Table 7>, the net inflow international migrants to Russia was about 100,000 per year in the mid-2000s, but has gradually increased since then, and now is maintaining about 250,000 to 300,000 annually in the 2010s. International residents in the Arctic region have also grown since the mid-2000s, maintaining a net inflow of about 10,000 to 13,000 people every year until now. In addition, ratio of the net inflow of international immigrants to the entire Russia to the ones to the Arctic region, the number is gradually rising from 1% in 2005 to 4% in 2012. This is an indication that the influx of international migrants into the Arctic region is steadily sustained despite the severe population outflow from Russian Arctic region. According to statistics from the 2016 Russian Population Yearbook, the net inflow of people from Ukraine is the largest in the Arctic region as a whole, along with the those from Tajikistan and Kyrgyzstan at a fairly high rate as well. (Росстат 2017a, Annex 7-7)

<Table 8> Trends of Foreign Workers in Russia (2000~2010, Unit: Person)

	2000	2002	2004	2005	2006	2007	2008	2009	2010
Russia	213,293	359,509	460,364	702,500	1,014,013	1,717,137	2,425,921	2,223,596	1,640,801
Karelia	1,092	6,807	2,524	2,743	2,187	3,315	4,669	2,827	2,042
Komi	1,297	4,050	1,358	4,050	2,961	4,377	5,840	6,329	5,537
Arkhangelsk	417	4,252	325	783	844	2,787	5,046	4,128	2,807
Nenets	68	1,671	514	1,162	1,582	2,804	2,881	2,684	2,230
Murmansk	409	5,053	708	1,559	1,453	2,672	3,632	4,112	4,574
Yamal	8,591	14,137	25,579	26,027	26,443	31,321	42,497	37,224	29,160
Krasnoyarsk	4,142	8,172	11,248	16,616	22,805	33,006	48,778	38,582	27,890
Sakha	958	1,789	6,336	10,624	14,861	19,427	21,966	15,427	17,672
Chukotka	425	-	4,458	4,934	4,451	5,126	5,093	3,974	2,680
Total	17,399	45,931	53,050	68,498	77,587	104,835	140,402	115,287	94,592
Percentage	8.2%	12.8%	11.5%	9.8%	7.7%	6.1%	5.8%	5.2%	5.8%

Source: the data for 2002 and 2004 were reconstructed from 'Russian Labor and Employment,' 2003: 298-300, 2005: 329-331. The data for other years were reconstructed from 'Russian Regional Social and Economic Indicators,' 2011: 128-129. Arkhangelsk and Nenets are calculated respectively. No data for 2001 and 2003.

Again, while natural population is growing in Russian Arctic region, the overall population is decreasing due to severe outflowing migration. But why are the international immigrants sustainably flowing in? This can be understood by looking at the situation of foreign workers in this region. Russia's National Statistical Office has been biannually publishing "Russian Labor and Employment" from 2003 to 2013, regarding the status of foreign workers by each Russian federal states (regional). And the circumstances have been provided every year since 2009 in "Russian Regional Social and Economic Indicators," where the statistics of year 2000 and the annual data from 2005 to 2017 are accumulated. <Table 8> summarizes the figures from 2000 to 2010 of these data. From the data of 2011, the annual "Russian Regional Social and Economic Indicators" distinguish the foreign labor workers into two: the acquirer of work permits and the acquirer of special labor certificates. <Table 9> that reconstructed the data of these two types of foreign workers from 2011 to 2017.

In the 1990s, there were approximately 200,000 foreign workers in Russia each year (Росстат 1999, 234) According to <Table 8>, this size was maintained until the early 2000s, with the number reaching over 1 million in the mid-2000s and over 2 million in the late 2000s. The factors affecting the increase or decrease in the number of foreign workers from various nationalities entering Russia are complex, therefore, it is quite difficult to explain the situation with only few reasons. However, it can be inferred that the most significant reason behind the increase in the number of foreign workers was the change in the Russian government's migration policy in 2005. At that time,

<Table 9> **Trends of Foreign Workers in Russia**

(2011~2017, Unit: Person / Total sum of acquirer of work permits and the acquirer of special labor certificates)

	2011	2013	2014	2015	2016	2017
Russia	1,792,829	2,229,327	3,123,606	1,838,658	1,687,317	1,764,075
Karelia	3,144	4,341	4,085	1,740	1,510	1,817
Komi	4,905	5,894	5,764	2,954	2,724	2,586
Arkhangelsk	2,930	2,695	3,200	1,785	1,712	1,909
Nenets	1,199	1,533	1,424	882	697	593
Murmansk	2,565	3,374	3,815	1,924	1,931	2,338
Yamal	19,014	27,274	27,792	15,125	12,757	11,569
Krasnoyarsk	35,479	32,788	42,206	24,784	21,350	22,608
Sakha	17,826	23,519	21,872	7,453	6,576	6,113
Chukotka	769	1,382	1,272	945	875	868
Total	87,831	102,800	111,430	57,592	50,132	50,401
Percentage	4.9%	4.6%	3.6%	3.1%	3.0%	2.9%

Source: the data were reconstructed from 'Russian Labor and Employment,' 2012: 144-145, 2016: 204-205, 2017: 218-221, 2018: 167-170. No data for 2012.

Putin recognized the population decline as a serious social problem, then decided to change Russia's foreign immigration policy by convening a special session of the Russian Federal Security Council. (специальное заседание Совета Безопасности РФ) The gist of the policy was not to leave the migrants unattended, but to gain their minds, so that they could settle in a new place, adapt to new conditions, and eventually integrate into Russian society. (Переведенцев 2007, 67; Ловцова и Ярская-Смирноваб 2005, 78-104) Then in July 2006, Putin signed an order to simplify the legal registration of labor migrants, and the bill went into effect in January 2007. (Малахов 2010, 151-158) Accordingly, foreign workers began to increase since the mid-2000s.

In the same sense, the foreign workers in the Arctic also increased in the 2000s. In the early 2000s, there were only 10,000 people, but in the mid-2000s, the number exceeded 50,000, and in the second half, it went over 100,000. A total of 38,512 international migrants were brought into Russian Arctic region over the five years from 2005 to 2009 (see <Table 7>), and 46,789 foreign workers increased from 68,498 in 2005 to 115,287 in 2009 (see <Table 8>). It can be inferred that a large number of the international migrants have entered Russia's Arctic region as foreign workers. However, among Russia's total foreign workers, the percentage of foreign workers in the Arctic region reached 11-12% in the early 2000s, but fell to 5-6% in the late 2000s. Nevertheless, the absolute figure of foreign workers steadily increased in the 2000s. Areas that had reached tens of thousands of people, especially due to the large number of foreign workers, include Yamal-Nenets, Krasnoyarsk, and Sakha. In the 2010s, the criteria for tallying foreign workers by Russia's National Statistics Office changed a bit, and as previously stated, it is reflected in <Table 9>. In Russia, the number of foreign workers increased to about 3.12 million in 2014, compared to about 1.8 million in 2011, but has since dwindled down to 1.76 million as of 2017. The reason for the sharp drop of foreign workers since 2014 can be attributed to Western economic sanctions against Russia. As Russia's economy deteriorated, the number of foreign workers was naturally reduced as companies closed or the number of unemployment increased. In Russian Arctic region, the number of foreign workers stood at about 110,000 in 2014, but has gone downsized to about 50,000 in 2017.

Among Russia's total foreign workers, the proportion of foreign workers in the Arctic also decreased, from about 5% in the early 2010s to about 3% in 2017. However, there are still about 12,000 international migrant net inflow per year to northern polar region of Russia, and the size of foreign workers remains at around 50,000. Till now, there are a number of foreign workers living in Yamal-Nenets and Krasnoyarsk. This shows that international migrants as foreign workers continue to flow in the region, despite the fact that the population continues to leak from the market reform period to the present.

V. Conclusion

The population of the Arctic region has declined by 1.92 million (20%), from about 9.72 million in 1990 to 7.8 million in 2017, and this trend is still going on to date. In fact, in the Arctic, the natural population has been growing since 2007, but the outflow of the population was on a larger scale which led the total number decreasing. Thus, the demographic situation in the Arctic region is quite negative.

Although natural growth of the population began in the mid-2000s in the Russian Arctic, the natural decline, which was taking place from the beginning of the 1990s to that point, left serious aftereffects. From the mid-2000s, the proportion of the working population began to decrease, from 67% in 2005 to 58% in 2017. This calculation presents the seriousness as it has fallen by a greater margin than Russia's overall average. Given the demographic situation of the internal population without considering the influx of people from the outside, it is estimated that it will be around 2030 that the ratio of working population in the Arctic region will be recovered. It is one of the achievements of this paper to sort out and forecast trends in the proportion of working population in the Russian Arctic.

Population leakage in the Russian Arctic is a serious social problem. In the 1990s and early 2000s, the average net outflow per 10,000 was over 100 people, and the average net outflow for each year from the mid- 2000s to 2017 was generally 50-80 per 10,000 people. At the same time, it should be noted that Russia's Arctic region is experiencing both inflow and oil output on a larger scale than other regions. However, the size of the outflow is larger, that the population is decreasing. Especially in the Arctic region, the ratio of population inflow and outflow is about two to three times higher than that of Russia as a whole. For Murmansk, Yamal-Nenets, and Chukotka, the rates of out-of-area migration are particularly high.

On the other hand, there is a steady net inflow of international migrants into Russia's Arctic region. The net inflow of international migrants into the Arctic region has remained at around 10,000 to 13,000 per year since the mid-2000s. In particular, there is a number of influx of immigrants from Ukraine, Tajikistan, and Kyrgyzstan, who are mostly foreign workers. In the mid-2000s, the number of foreign workers and international migrants began to increase in Russia's Arctic region due to eased regulations, maintaining around 100,000 per year.

Since 2014, however, the number of foreign workers has been reduced to about 50,000 due to worsening economic conditions in Russia which followed after Western economic sanctions. However, though the foreign workers' scale in Yamal-Nenets, Krasnoyarsk, and Sakha got smaller, there are still a considerable number of them. In recent years, the population has been increasing gradually in these areas. Despite the continued outflow of the population as a whole, international migrants as foreign workers are sustainably flowing into the Arctic region of Russia. They are not only slow the pace of population decline in the region, but also are important human resources to fill the lack of working population. The analysis of statistical information on the inflow of international migrants and foreign workers and the assessment that they can be important human resources in the region is one of the major achievements of this paper as well.

The study has its significance in that Russia's Arctic region was categorized as one independent unit to analyze population and migration trends. It is also significant that 30 years of statistical data accumulated after the market reform period could be used to more objectively to track the trends in demographic characteristics in the Arctic. Based on the analysis of demographic characteristics for the Russia's Arctic region, it is necessary to pursue detailed research in the future, including comparative studies and typing among Arctic regions or analysis on specific causes for demographic phenomena captured in the individual regions.

Reference

Choi, Wooik. “The Population Decline and the Influx of the International Immigrants in Russia – the Problem of Human Resources.” *Journal of North-East Asian Cultures*(The Association on North-east Asian Cultures), V. 26 (2011).

Choi, Wooik. “Socio-Economic Changes and Characteristics of Arctic People in Russia.” *Russian Studies*(Seoul National University), V. 28. № 1 (2018). Han, Jong-Man et al. *Understanding the Russian Arctic Circle*(Seoul: Shinasa, 2010).

Je, Sung Hoon, Min, Jiyoung. “Russian Arctic Development Strategy and New Possibility for Korea-Russia Cooperation.” *Studies in Comprehensive Regional Strategies*(KIEP), 13-08 (2013).

Young, T. Kue and Peter Bjerregaard. *Health Transition in Arctic Populations* (Toronto: University of Toronto Press Incorporated, 2007).

Ловцова, Н. И. и Е. Р. Ярская-Смирнова. “Демогафическая проблема: кто винават и что делать?” *Мир России*, № 4 (2005).

Макар, С. В. “Векторы пространственного развития Арктической зоны России.” *Российская Арктика – территория права* (Москва-Салехард: Юриспруденция, 2015).

Малахов, В. С. “Иммиграционные режимы в государствах запада и в России: теоретико-политический аспект.” *ПОЛИС*, № 4 (2010).

Переведенцев, В. И. “Демогафические перспективы России.” *СОЦИС*, № 12 (2007).

Подвинцев, О. Б. и др. *Российская Арктика в пойсках интегральной идентичности* (Москва: Новый хронограф, 2016).

Ревичи, Б. А. *Демографические процессы, динамика трудовых ресурсов и риски здоровью населения европейской части Арктической зоны*

России (Москва: ЛЕНАНД, 2016).
Силин, А. Н. *Социальные проблемы Арктического региона* (Тюмень: ТИУ, 2016).
Росстат. *Труд и занятость в России* (Москва: Росстат, 1999).
Росстат. *Демографический ежегодник России* (Москва: Росстат, 2001a).
Росстат. *Регионы России. Социально-экономические показатели* (Москва: Росстат, 2001b).
Росстат. *Труд и занятость в России* (Москва: Росстат, 2003).
Росстат. *Демографический ежегодник России* (Москва: Росстат, 2005a).
Росстат. *Труд и занятость в России* (Москва: Росстат, 2005b).
Росстат. *Демографический ежегодник России* (Москва: Росстат, 2006).
Росстат. *Демографический ежегодник России* (Москва: Росстат, 2007).
Росстат. *Демографический ежегодник России* (Москва: Росстат, 2008).
Росстат. *Демографический ежегодник России* (Москва: Росстат, 2009).
Росстат. *Демографический ежегодник России* (Москва: Росстат, 2010a).
Росстат. *Регионы России. Социально-экономические показатели* (Москва: Росстат, 2010b).
Росстат. *Регионы России. Социально-экономические показатели* (Москва: Росстат, 2011).
Росстат. *Демографический ежегодник России* (Москва: Росстат, 2012a).
Росстат. *Регионы России. Социально-экономические показатели* (Москва: Росстат, 2012b).
Росстат. *Демографический ежегодник России* (Москва: Росстат, 2013a).
Росстат. *Регионы России. Социально-экономические показатели* (Москва: Росстат, 2013b).
Росстат. *Демографический ежегодник России* (Москва: Росстат, 2014a).
Росстат. *Регионы России. Социально-экономические показатели* (Москва: Росстат, 2014b).

Росстат. *Демографический ежегодник России* (Москва: Росстат, 2015a).

Росстат. *Регионы России. Социально-экономические показатели* (Москва: Росстат, 2015b).

Росстат. *Российский статический ежегодник* (Москва: Росстат, 2015c).

Росстат. *Регионы России. Социально-экономические показатели* (Москва: Росстат, 2016a).

Росстат. *Российский статический ежегодник* (Москва: Росстат, 2016b).

Росстат. *Демографический ежегодник России* (Москва: Росстат, 2017a).

Росстат. *Регионы России. Социально-экономические показатели* (Москва: Росстат, 2017b).

Росстат. *Регионы России. Социально-экономические показатели* (Москва: Росстат, 2018).

Arctic Megapedia. "Арктическая зона Российской Федерации." http://arctic-megapedia.ru/wiki/Арктическая_зона_Российской_Федерации(retrieved on 2018.03.02.).

Политобразование. Арктическая зона Российской Федерации(АЗРФ). http://lawinrussia.ru/content/arkticheskaya-zona-rossiyskoy-federacii-azrf(retrieved on 2018.03.17.).

Районный крайнего севера России. https://yandex.ru/images/search?text=районный_крайнего_севера_россии(retrieved on 2018.03.02.).

Северный (Арктический) федеральный университет. Российская Арктика или Арктическая зона?. http://narfu.ru/aan/Encyclopedia_Arctic/RA-AZRF.PDF(retrieved on 2016.07.02.).

Федеральная служба государственной статистики. Перечень районов Крайнего Севера и приравненных к ним местностей на 1 января 2009 года. http://www.gks.ru/bgd/regl/b0922/isswww.exe/stg/territoriya.htm (retrieved on 2018.03.14.).

The Landscape of Deconstruction:

Visual Representations of the Arctic in Contemporary Russian Cinema

Seungdo Ra

I. Introduction

Russia's extraordinary interest on the Arctic, since the collapse of the Soviet Union in 1991, is particularly noticeable during the reign of President Vladimir Putin, who has been in office for nearly 20 years since 2000. This is clearly implied in the establishment and implementation of national policies for Arctic management and development, including 1) the 'Russian Federal Arctic Basic Policy 2020' signed by Putin in 2008, 2) the Presidential decree 296 'Russian Federation Arctic Territory,' which went into effect in May 2014, and 3) the 'The Arctic Territory Expansion' Act, which was approved in 2018. (Staalesen, 2019)

In addition, the Russian government has hosted the international forum 'The Arctic: Territory of Dialogue' on five irregular occasions so far in Moscow, Salekhard, Arkhangelsk, and St. Petersburg until 2019. In November of the same year, the 'Moscow Arctic Day' was first held under the auspices of the Russian Geographic Society, currently directed by Putin, chaired by Defense Minister Sergei Shoigu, and hosted by the Ministry of Natural Resources and Environment. This particular day has been held every year ever since. The organizers declare that the purpose of the event is to arouse people's interest in the Arctic's nature, history, and culture. Above all, one effective method they are using for the 'Arctic Day' is the active utilization of the film media. This is one of the main 'Moscow Arctic Day' events, which is why 'Arctic Film Festival' or 'Arctic Film Watching' are always taking a part of the day.

What's more interesting is that the number of recent visual artworks regarding the Arctic in the Russian film industry also first increased in 2010, when the 'The Arctic: Territory of Dialogue' international forum and 'Arctic Day' began to be established and held. In fact, Aleksei Popogrebskii's *How I Ended This Summer* (Как я провел этим летом) was released in 2010 and became Russia's first post-Soviet era Arctic film. The year 2014 was followed by numerous films which had significant value in terms of creativity and current affairs, such as Andrei Zviagintsev's *Leviathan* (Левиафан), Nataliia Meshchaninova's *'Hope' Factory* (Комбинат 'Надежда'), Vladimir Tumayev's *White Yagel* (Белый ягель), and Alexandr Mel'nik's Territory (Территория).

Soon after, Philip Abriutin's *The Tragedy of Rodgers Bay* (Трагедия в бухте Роджерс) based on a true story in the 1930s, continued to focus on the Arctic in Russian films. In 2017, the film *The First* (Первые), which dealt with Semyon Cheliuskin who explored the Arctic in 18th century, backcasted Russia' s story of its exploration and conquest of the North Pole. Finally, in 2019, Ginaida Longortova, an indigenous Russian Arctic minority, showed the Khanty ethnicity's performance during World War II from the perspective of minorities themselves through *Khon Iush. Path from the Ob* (Хон юш. Путь от Оби). But the visual representation of the Arctic in Russian films in the 2010s does not just end up with film dramas. Even in documentary films, the Arctic has been an important object which stayed between memories and records. For example, Aleksei Vakhrushev's *The Tundra Book: A Tale of Vukvukai, The Little Rock* (Книга тундры: Повесть о Вуквукае — маленьком камне, 2011) describes the real story of a 72-year old man's life who raises reindeer in the Chukotka tundra in the northern Russia.

Similarly, Dmitri Lavrinenko's *Children of the Tundra* (Дети тундры) which was played on the 'Moscow Arctic Day' in 2014, tells the story of the tundra minority Nenets' children who live all the way from the Murmansk Kola Peninsula to the Krasnoyarsk Taymyr Peninsula. Meanwhile, *Three Expeditions. Russian Arctic Region* (Три капитана. Русская арктика), created in 2013 by Maxim Feitelberg and screened in 2014 "Arctic Day," traces the great deeds of Russian explorers who have succeeded in conquering the North Pole and exploring the Arctic route, including Georgii Sedov. In 2018,

Leonid Govorov's *Great Journey to the Arctic* follows the so-called Northern Route of the explorer Semyon Dezhnyov who extended the boundaries of the Russian empire to the Far East in the 17th century.

Another important phenomenon in the visual reproduction of the Arctic is the fact that some parts of Russia's Arctic areas have recently established and held annual Arctic themed film festivals. For example, the Khanty-Mansiisk autonomous district is hosting an international film festival focusing on its debut film, since 2003, under the title of 'The Spirit of Fire (Дух огня).'

In addition, the Sakha Republic established the first 'Arctic Film' festival in local level as well as Yakut International Film Festival, which annually invites local and foreign filmmakers, since 2013. Furthermore, the Chukotka autonomous district has established the International Arctic Film Festival under the title of 'Golden Crow (Золотой ворон)' in 2017, which is held annually in Anadyr,' the capital of the region. In the same year, Arkhangelsk also began holding the 'Artic Open' international film festival, which has purpose in building networks among Arctic related movie artists all together. As many parts of Russia's Arctic regions competitively launch Arctic themed film festivals recently, the visual representation of the Arctic has become more actively productive.

The interest in the Arctic, which rises over the years in Russia, can also be clearly seen in the visual representation process of the Arctic in the Russian film industry. However, research that details the visual representation of the Arctic in post-Soviet era Russian films is rarely seen so far, especially on Putin's reign over the past two decades. (Sarkisova 2019, 231-253) Therefore, serious research on the visual representation of the Arctic, which appears in many colors in Russian films during the post-Soviet era, is urgently needed as the importance of the Arctic has been growing not only in Russia but throughout the world as well. With the aim of filling this research vacuum, this paper will make an analysis of the visual representation patterns and cultural implications of the Arctic, focusing on major works that occupy special positions in the post-Soviet era Russian Arctic Cinema.

II. Russian 'Arctic Cinema' and the Landscape of Deconstruction

In 1990, a year before the collapse of the Soviet Union, there were 300 Russian films. However, the number of movies plunged as the Russian film industry was hit hard by the suspension of state funding right after the collapse of the Soviet Union. Less than five years after the collapse of the Soviet Union, only 46 films were made in 1995. (Graffy 1998, 190) However, of course, a sharp decline in the number of movie production does not mean that good works have not been produced.

Nikita Mikhalkov's *Burnt by the Sun* (Утомленные Солнцем) which was released in 1994, has also gained international fame as he has contributed greatly to the reevaluation of Stalin's legacy that swept through the 1990s, winning the Academy Award for Best International Feature Film. Also, among the films produced during the ideological vacuum in the 1990s after the collapse of socialism, quite a number of films devoted to the search for new national ideas and collective identity of Russia during the post-Soviet era.

With the Russian film industry changing rapidly after the collapse of the Soviet Union, covering the Arctic space in film was more like a luxury. While the exotic images of the Caucasus were diversely appearing in Russian films due to the influence of the First and Second Chechen Wars, the visual images of the Arctic could not be found at all in Russian films in the 1990s. In other words, the Arctic was not a major concern to both the national and film levels at the time. This has not changed much even till the 21st century.

There were no particular Russian "Arctic Film" in the 2000s, except for *Under the Polaris* by Maksim Voronkov, which was screened as a five episode TV soap opera in 2002. At the Russian government level, the Arctic policy and discourse only began to emerge in earnest in the late 2000s, as the Russian Federal Arctic Basic Policy 2020 was published in 2008. In short, Russia's interest in the Arctic was not so prominent in the 1990s and even in 2000s. The reason that Arctic films in Russian movie industry did not really take a part before the 2010s, was also related to such situation that Russian government and society were not fully recognizing the importance of the Arctic and that the image of the Arctic was not widely seen. (Sarkisova 2019, 237-238)

1. *How I Ended This Summer*

In the 2010s, however, as Russian society started to give attention to the Arctic, the 'Arctic Revolution' of Russian cinema began to take off; because Aleksei Popogrebskii's *How I Ended This Summer* was released in 2010. In this regard, Popogrebskii's film can be defined as the first Russian 'Arctic film' of the post-Soviet era. However, though his film first showcased images of the Arctic in Russia after the collapse of the Soviet Union, the visual representation of the Arctic and its significance are more likely to have strong connection to the so-called 'Red Arctic' myth established in the 1930s Stalinist culture as a whole.

How I Ended This Summer can be seen in the context of the 'Soviet Nostalgia' which stands out during Putin's reign, given that it presents the first Arctic space in the post-Soviet era and is further linked to the Soviet 'Arctic myth.' However, unlike the expectation, this film undermines and deconstructs rather than inherits the Arctic myth of the Soviet cinema.

For example, in Sergei Gerasimov's North Pole exploration movie

Seven Brave Men (Семеро смелых) in 1936, the Arctic is dominated by 'the landscape of heroism,' which is characterized by the Stalinist culture of the 1930s (Maccannon 2003, 255). Here, the Arctic is a mythical space where Soviet explorers and scientists successfully complete numerous missions with superhuman powers, overcoming all kinds of trials and adversity with indomitable determination, like positive heroes of socialist realism. Moreover, in Gerasimov's film, the Arctic extends its meaning to an ideal living environment that explodes the potential of self-realization as the main characters engage in a variety of activities. (Bugaeva 2015, 310-324)

However, in Popogrebsk'i's movie, the Arctic is more likely described as the space of coward behavior rather than a mythical place where heroism is played out. In short, *How I Ended This Summer* is of special value as Russia's first post-Soviet era Arctic film, but at the same time it also has significant meaning as a film that breaks up and overthrows the Soviet era Arctic myth.

In Popogrebskii's film, the main event occurs with the uncomfortable and unstable relationship between two men working at the weather station on a northernmost remote island in Chukotka autonomous district. One of them is a middle-aged man in his 50s, Sergei Guliabin, the head of weather station. He quietly undertakes the mission of collecting and recording weather data observed in the station and reports them daily to the mainland weather center. The other is a young man in his 20s, Pavel Danilov, an intern for the summer at a weather station. These two men contrast in many ways from the very beginning of the movie. First of all, there is a clear generation gap between the two. These differences can be seen in their appearance, attire, way of talk, and behavior. Sergei is big-built and reticent. On the other hand, Pavel, like usual young man, wanders around the station and always listens to music with headphones regardless he is working or resting. At the same time, he is often engrossed in computer games when he is resting in the shelter. In this regard, Pavel, as the new generation who just came from outside the island, represents the post-Soviet era, while the Sergei represents the Soviet era as an old generation isolated inside the island. (Lipovetsky & Mikhailova 2010; Strukov 2012, 19-45)

What should be noted here is that the generational conflict between Sergei and Pavel extends into a conflict between the Soviet era and the post-Soviet era. However, these times of conflict are also illustrated by the so-called 'Arctic discourse,' which is implied in the movie's narrative. As noted earlier, Soviet-era films on the Arctic always present the main character as a way of overcoming obstacles and accomplishing missions under any circumstances and challenges. In this process, the elder often sets an example to younger people, and the younger obeys by following his instructions or guidance. In other words, this film also presented the figure of a positive hero, a key feature of Soviet socialist realism, described as a true hero and leader who is loved and respected by his subordinates. In addition, in Soviet era Arctic films, the main characters always believe in the spirit of collectivism rather than individualism.

But in *How I Ended This Summer*, not only as the head of the weather station but also as an elder, without receiving any respect or care from Pavel, Sergei has a strange sense of distance and even hostility. In the scene where Sergei and Pavel enjoy sauna, they temporarily transcend the generation gap and the vertical relationship by sharing masculine bond with strength, bravery, and patience. However, the tension and conflict arising from their awkward relationship reach the climax when Pavel fails to tell Sergei the grievous news from the superior office, which was Sergei's wife and son's death. Pavel and Sergei eventually cannot narrow the gap of misunderstanding through dialogue or form a relationship of mutual understanding and harmony, but they rather avoid each other and in the end fall into the abyss of distrust and discord. In addition, Pavel is trapped in guilt which comes from Sergei's family's death and his impending death. Because Pavel let Sergei eat radioactive salmon, he could not escape from the guilt complex. In this sense, it is quite ironic that in the end Pavel get on board the helicopter, leaving only Sergei alone on a remote island in the Arctic.

Popogrebskii's film shows the breakdown of human relations through the stories of Sergei and Pavel, while further suggesting the collapse of the Soviet Arctic myth that began in Gerasimov's films. The first post-Soviet Arctic film, *How I Ended This Summer*, mysteriously overturns the Arctic discourse presented in Gerasimov's *Seven Brave Men*, the first and prototype of the Soviet Arctic films. Gerasimov's film has Arctic's winter as a background. It shows seven brave men completing their mission in winter by overcoming the harsh natural conditions of the Arctic, like one family. They are all different across occupations and gender, including scientists, pilots, men and women, but such differences do not hinder their human relations and mission performance. They show the perfect image of heroic achievement (подвиг) by becoming 'one' in challenging circumstances and overcoming all adversities. As shown in <Figure 1> and <Figure 2>, their winter hut zimovka (зимовка) presents the warm family and pastoral atmosphere that keeps them together. Outside the cabin is dominated by the harsh nature of the Arctic, but inside is just warm with decent food, joyful music, and intellectual feeling. The hut even carries out surgery on patients from the Arctic minority. All of these are metaphorical images of an ideal new world built with Soviet modernity in the Arctic.

<Figure 1> <Figure 2>

But all these idealistic images completely go the opposite in Popogrebskii's *How I Ended This Summer*. First, as the title suggests, the film is set in summer, not winter, and Pavel and Sergei stay at the weather station instead of zimovka. Furthermore, though only two of them are staying, just a few scenes show them preparing and eating meals together, unlike *Seven Brave Men*. There were a couple of momentary atmosphere of reconciliation between them, such as when they were together in sauna or when they were washing the fish that Sergei caught. However, there is always a peculiar tension between them. Pavel usually spends his time playing video games when he's alone, while Sergei's out on patrol around the island or for fishing. In addition, Pavel is quite clumsy with his duties that Sergei frequently needs to scold and nag at him. Expecting a family relation between them in a symbolic sense is very near to impossible. Moreover, when Pavel received the telegram that Sergei's family died in an accident, it suggests the actual dissolution of the family, but at the same time it also implies the breakup of the symbolic family.

Pavel was not brave enough to deliver this disastrous news to Sergei, so he disappears without a trace all of sudden. Later, as Sergei concerned Pavel, he grabs a gun and starts looking for Pavel, but Pavel thinks Sergei might kill him so runs away farther and farther. What's noteworthy here is the scene of an abandoned cabin on a coastal cliff where Pavel hides from Sergei. Instead of going back to the weather station, Pavel sets on fire in the stove, melts himself and sleeps in an old bed. As shown in <Figure 3>, the smoke rising from the chimney as Pavel sets fire to the stove reminds us that it was actually a cozy and warm pastoral space before it became as ruined as it is shown. However, <Figure 4> shows that this is only a tensed place of crisis in the relationship between Sergei and Pavel, who are chasing and being chased. In other words, the cottage is not exactly what you see in Soviet era Arctic movies, but a place dominated by a threatening atmosphere that destroys human relationships, rather than a warm family atmosphere among people.

<Figure 3> **<Figure 4>**

What's more interesting is that as seen in <Figure 4>, Pavel's game has shifted to the reality exactly the same: chasing and being chased, killing and being killed. In the video game, Pavel becomes a pursuer to find and kill enemies hiding in abandoned buildings like his cottage in the real life. In reality, however, Pavel is hiding in extreme tension in this abandoned cabin, escaping from armed Sergei. In addition, in

Pavel's video game, the tracker finds and tries to kill enemies lurking in abandoned buildings, but eventually in the end, the chaser enters a radioactive zone and then dies. In this scenario, while Pavel plays the role of the tracker in the virtual reality of the video game, in the real world, Sergei who chase after Pavel takes on the role of the tracker.

Also in the real world, it's not Pavel who dies due to radioactive contamination. In short, the virtual reality of video games and the real world of the main characters are much alike, but as a major role reverses between the two worlds, the 'landscape of heroism' characteristic of the 'Arctic myth' in Soviet cinema is also dismantled. Instead of making 'heroic' moves in the post-Soviet Arctic space, Pavel not only kills Sergei with his 'anti-heroic' cowardice, but also falls into moral and ethical death himself.

In *How I Ended This Summer*, the visual representation of the Arctic does not really show the 'mythic landscape of heroism' in which the characters complete their mission as they band together into human and family bonds to confront the challenges. The film, on the other hand, shows the aspect of failed and dissolved myths where the remains of Soviet modernity are piled up.

The oil barrels, nuclear power facilities, and abandoned buildings like the huts on coastal cliff near the weather station only bring up the gloomy view of disintegration and degradation. With this approach, Popogrebskii implicitly emphasizes that the Soviet propaganda of ideally realizing the idyllic life does not function in the post-Soviet

Arctic space, which is dominated by harsh natural environments. In the film, the Arctic is a place that represents isolation, solitude, and silence, while death stays everywhere as can be inferred from the scenes of radiation exposure. In this regard, Popogrebskii's film can be interpreted as a challenge to the Soviet film's 'Arctic discourse' and a way of deconstruction.

2. *Leviathan*

As we have confirmed so far, the Arctic in post-Soviet Russian films is overwhelmed by the gloomy perspectives of ruins and disintegration, where only the old image of Soviet modernity remains. Interestingly, this visual reenactment is also evident in Andrei Zvyagintsev's *Leviathan*, released in 2014. The desolate landscape along the coast of Russia's northernmost Kola Peninsula near the Barents Sea was presented in the introduction and the end of the film as well as the abandoned ships that evoke the image of giant dead animals delivering loneliness and desertedness. Zvyagintsev chose Teriberka, the northernmost Russian Arctic port town of the Kola Peninsula, for his movie.

Teriberka was settled in 1927 and began to flourish in the 1950s as the Arctic fishing industry grew. As the recent study shows, the influence of Soviet modernity has extended to the remote Arctic areas as industries developed in Teriberka, the population grew significantly, and modern buildings of neoclassicism style started to spread in everywhere. (Olsen & Vinogradova 2019, 1-18) But when Russia's economy was at its worst in the 1990s after the Soviet Union collapsed in 1991, Teriberka was also hit directly by the economic downturn and many places went empty as its population declined rapidly. As a result, the post-Soviet Teriberka entered "an entropic process of discomposition" (Larsen & Hemmersam 2017, 177), which Zvyagintsev desired to capture and emphasize in *Leviathan*: the view of disintegration and ruins in Teriberka.

<Figure 5>

The wreckage of the ship in Teriberka as shown in <Figure 5> is a stark reminder of the devastation of the Arctic, but also of the painful memories of the political persecution during the Stalin era. (Vassilieva 2017, 36) In the 1920s, Teriberka had one of the Stalin era's labor camps (GULAG) which were built on the Russian Arctic areas in Kola

Peninsula. Those imprisoned in the camp were mobilized mainly for fishing based on the Barents Sea. The wrecked ships, repeatedly presented at the beginning and end of the film, were the ones used by those prisoners. In this way of approach, Zvyagintsev recalls historical memories of political persecution, carved in Soviet era arctic spaces, as an important part of the post-Soviet 'Arctic discourse.' Just in this respect, Zvyagintsev's *Leviathan* forms a clear contrast to Sergei Gerasimov's *Seven Brave Men* and *City of Youth* (Город юности, 1938) and Aleksei Simonov's *Ordinary Arctic* (Обыкновенная Арктика, 1974). These Soviet era Arctic films praise the heroic efforts of those who devote themselves to building new lives in the Arctic. However, they remain silent about the stories of victims of political persecution mobilized in the construction of Arctic industrial cities such as Vorkuta of Komi Republic and Norilsk in Krasnoyarsk region. In this regard, Zvyagintsev's *Leviathan* can be defined as the first film of the Soviet and post-Soviet era which hauled the history of forced labor and political persecution within the Arctic from the darkness.

Leviathan tells the story of a dramatic reversal of the unexpected misfortune faced by Nikolai, his wife and son, set in a small fishing port town on the coast of the Barents Sea in the Russian Arctic. The middle-aged Nicolai lives with his remarried wife Liliia and middle-school son Roma, running a car garage in a coastal house he inherited from his parents. This family, however, has tension and conflict between the parents and son, as Liliia and Roma frequently quarrel.

Already with the existing domestic issue, the conflict grows bigger from an individual level to a power structure as the mayor designates Nikolai's house as the redevelopment area and plans to build a church. Then the family meets a larger crisis of disintegration again. The dark shadow of this misfortune is led to the overall disintegration of human relations surrounding Nikolai, who is shaped as the post-Soviet era's 'Little Man.' (Wengle 2018, 1017)

Interestingly in *Leviathan*, one of the means that mediates the interpersonal communication and relations is vodka. The main narrative of *Leviathan* begins with a scene of Dmitrii, who works as a lawyer in Moscow, arriving in a local city by train to help his troubled military colleague Nikolai. Nicolai and Dmitrii are close friends since they were in the army. This relationship is presented in a constant manner even though they meet again after a long time since they were discharged. Their steadfast friendship is illustrated in several scenes where they drink vodka in and out of season when they meet again. Again, their close relationship can be interpreted that it gets intensified with alcohol. Nicolai and Dimitri sometimes enjoy vodka in Nikolai's house and reminisce about their past, but they also hang out with multiple people outside the house drinking vodka.

Nikolai and Dmitrii, for example, go on a picnic with a neighbor Ivan Stefanych for his birthday, and have non-stopping vodka shots when they play shooting as shown in <Figure 6>. At this party, there were traffic cop Pasha and his wife Angelina, who all came together in one and mingled naturally, thanks to vodka again. Here vodka dilutes the differences among people and brings up a collective homogeneity. Vodka is shown as an important mechanism that keeps people's relationships smooth at any place and time. In other words, as seen in the scene which four men drinking quite seriously before they start shooting, vodka somewhat expresses and emphasizes the masculine homogeneity or bond. (Seungdo Ra, 2015, 52-53)

<Figure 6>

As described above, vodka was representing the function of smoothing the connections and human relationships, but on the other hand, it later introduces the adverse effect in terms of the fact that it put the relations into a crisis of dissolution. In the picnic scene, Nikolai and Pasha's family were chilling out after the shooting match, while suddenly but secretly Nikolai's wife Liliia leaves the spot. Following her, Dmitrii also carefully heads to somewhere, where apparently Liliia and Dimitrii cross the line that should not be. Two were enjoying the physical relationship, but soon were caught.

Later, due to this happening Nikolai and Dmitrii have a serious fistfight then eventually turn into a hostile relationship. The relationship between the two friends walks toward the process of disintegration. Moreover, Nikolai's life is ruined as his wife Liliia disappears all of sudden without leaving any trace. He binges drinking vodka every day with anxiety and nervousness until later Liliia was found dead on the beach. As such, the image of dismantling dominates not only the natural scenery of coastal villages in the Arctic, but also the physical and mental aspects of people living there.

However, *Leviathan* sparked strong criticism from Russian conservatives and government officials due to such frequent imbibing vodka scenes, where most of the characters including the wicked mayor are drinking during the whole film. They deplored that *Leviathan* has destroyed Russian society's positive aspect but only described the negatives which are soaked in vodka and filled with abusive language. Russian Culture Minister Vladimir Medinskii directly criticized that no matter how high *Leviathan* is in the reviews, he personally doesn't like the movie at all, because there were too many abusive and heavy drinking scenes. In addition, he also pointed out that there is no 'positive' character in the entire film.

Medinskii's comments, on the other hand, indirectly support the fact that *Leviathan* is boldly breaking up the 'landscape of heroism' of Soviet Arctic films which are normally filled with positive characters. (Zviagintsev 2018)

III. Conclusion

Nataliia Meshchaninova's *'Hope' Factory*, which was released in the same year of Zvyagintsev's *Leviathan*, has its set in Norilsk, a Krasnoyarsk frontier built by victims of political persecution, like Teriberka in the Kola Peninsula. Like *Leviathan*, it also suggests the serious social problems that Russian Arctic regions are facing today.

For example, in this movie, teenagers in Norilsk drink vodka and curse at each other whenever they hang out together, just as the abusive language and binge drinking may make their relationships stronger. In addition, as the relationship between young main character and her parents demonstrates, the generation gap and conflict are described as reaching a serious level. Moreover, just like the main character, young people in the film seek for a chance to leave Norilsk because they feel like this isolated area makes them suffocated. Ironically, the message of 'hope' in the title of the film, which is also the name of the world's largest nickel-producing factory in Norilsk, has been turned into a message of 'despair' by a female figure with the same name as the factory named 'Nadezhda' drowning in the film's later parts.

As such, the representative works of 'Arctic cinema,' newly showcased during the post-Soviet era in the 2010s, emphasize the 'landscape of deconstruction," overturning the 'Arctic discourse' established during the Soviet era. Along with this, as seen in *Leviathan*, historical memories of political persecution, which has been ignored or tabooed, have also begun to form an important part in modern Russian Arctic films.

This new change is a great significance in that it has opened the door for us to seek a wise solution to the problems facing us in the Arctic area today, presenting another 'landscape of deconstruction,' such as forced resettlement and collectivization of the Arctic indigenous people, and environmental pollution and destruction. It is particularly encouraging that a series of films portray the problems of the minority nationalities in the Arctic from their own perspective, such as the aforementioned *Khon* Iush. Path from the Ob. Therefore, the introduction and analysis of these films also need to be done seriously.

Reference

Bugaeva, Lyubov. "'Here will be a Garden-City': Soviet Man on an Arctic Construction Site." Scott MacKenzie & Anna Westerståhl Stenport (eds.), \ *Films on Ice: Cinemas of the Arctic: Traditions in World Cinema.* (Edinburgh: Edinburgh University Press, 2015).

Graffy, Julian. "Cinema," Catriona Kelly and David Shepherd (ed), *Rusian Cultural Studies: An Introduction* (Cambridge: Cambridge University Press, 1998).

Hemmersam, P and Larsen, J. (2017). "Landscapes on Hold: The Norwegian and Russian Barents Sea Coast in the New North". In *Critical Norths: Space, Nature, Theory*. Fairbanks: University of Alaska Press.

Maccannon, John. "Tabula Rasa in the North: The Soviet Arctic and Mythic Landscapes in Stalinist Popular Culture." Evgeny Dobrenko and Eric Naiman (ed), *The Landscape of Stalinism: The Art and Ideology of Soviet Space* (Seattle: University of Washington Press, 2003).

Olsen, Bjørnar Julius & Vinogradova, Svetlana. "(In)significantly Soviet: the Heritage of Teriberka." *Journal International Journal of Heritage Studies*, Vol. 82, No. 2 (2019).

Ra, Seungdo (2015). "Leviathan: A Duet of the Intimate and the Unfamiliar." *Russia & Russian Federation*, Vol. 6, No. 1.

Sarkisova, Oksana. "Moving Through the Century: The Far North in Soviet and Contemporary Russian Nonfiction." Lilya Kaganovsky, Scott MacKenzie and Anna Westerstahl Stenport (eds.). *Arctic Cinemas and the Documentary Ethos* (Bloomington: Indiana University Press, 2019).

Staalesen, Atle. "Russia's Far East Ministry to Get Powers over Arctic policy." *The Independent Barents Observer* (January 21, 2019).

Strukov, Vlad. "Ludic Digitality: A. Sokurov's *Russian Ark* and A.

Popogrebskii's *How I Ended This Summer* as Cinegames." *Digital Icons: Studies in Russian, Eurasian and Central European New Media*, No 8 (2012).

Vassilieva, Julia. "Russian Leviathan: Power, Landscape, Memory." *Film Criticism*, Vol. 42, No. 1 (2018).

Wengle, Susanne. "Russia's Post-Soviet Ideological Terrain - Zvygintsev's Leviathan and Debates on Authority, Agency, and Authenticity." *Slavic Review*, Vol. 77, No. 4 (2018).

Zviagintsev, Andrei (2018). "Ia ne dumaiu o zritele voobshche. Eto poslednee, o chem tvorcheskii chelovekdolzhen dumat'". https://republic.ru/posts/90357

The Policies for the Indigenous Minority Peoples in Russia

Bongchul Kim & Minkyung Shin

I. Introduction

In the case of Russia, various 'aboriginal ethnicities' were absorbed as the its territory expanded. In Central Asia, there was China to the East; the Huns, Gokturks, and Mongols to the North; India to the Southeast; and Persia to the Southwest; becoming a melting pot of civilizations. Since then, due to various historical rationales, Russia has become an area of geopolitical peculiarities where all civilizations converge.

The meaning of "Indigenous and minority peoples" in the global society, both economically and culturally, is never light. As also, the Minority Peoples have an important meaning in the aspects of politics, economy, culture, and society. Russia is the representative country where multiracial nation with 180 and 130 Peoples live together. The number of these ethnic groups reach approximately 400,000, which is less than 0.3% of the entire Russian population, however, the absolute number is never small. There are officially total 277 languages that are used in Russia, as the Constitution Article 68 says "the republics shall have the right to establish their own state languages" while Russian is the official language for the entire Russian Federation; nonetheless more than two thirds have no opportunity to be educated in schools.

According to the Russian Government Resolution No. 255, *Abazin, Aleut, Alutorts, Besermyan, Veps, Vod,' Dolgan, Izhorc, Itelmen, Camchadal, Kerek, Ket, Koryak, Kumandints, Mansi, Nagaibak, Nanaits, Nganasan, Negidalts, Nenets, Nivh, Orok, Oroch, Sami, Selkup, Soyot, Taz, Telengit, Teleut, Tofalar, Tubalar, Tuvints-todzhits, Udygeits, Ulchi, Hant, Chelkan, Chuvants, Chukchi, Evenk, Even, Ents, Eskimo,* and *Yukagir* are listed as the Indigenous Small Peoples of Russia. The Russian law indicates 'small in number' as the not exceeding 50,000.

These Peoples have long received special attention from the Russian government, and their meaning has become more significant since the dissolution of the Soviet Union. Recently, however, the focus on these groups has shifted from mere economical subjects to a crucial member of global and cultural diversity, or those most vulnerable to environmental issues such as global warming. The major concerns of violation on indigenous minority's right embrace discrimination, xenophobia, abuse of law, prejudice, and so on.

Numerous international organizations have been established in order to resolve relevant issues with minority groups, and many multiracial countries are also paying attention to their aboriginals and minorities, respectively. Russia is making various efforts to support their minority groups by forming lists and providing special legal status. Despite speculations that the list is not solely intended for the protection of minorities, it represents that the Russian government is aware of the need for special care and support of these minorities.

The main purpose of this study is to organize and analyze policies related to indigenous peoples and minorities in Russia and through this information to find out the meaning it has in modern society. So for this purpose, the concept and status of the Indigenous Minority Peoples in Russia is analyzed as the basic approach to the topic. Then, it examines the policies of the government to protect the rights especially in the sphere of international and domestic legislation. Finally, the limitations and problems of the Policies in Russia are analyzed from two perspectives, legal system and ethnic identity.

In order to carry out this paper, the primary data such as documents related to the Russian Federal Law will be used. It also conducted statistical analysis through institutional and government reports related with Indigenous and Minority Peoples in Russia from the days of the Soviet Union to the present governments.

II. Concept and status of the indigenous peoples and ethnic minorities in Russia

1. International definition: Indigenous peoples and Ethnic minorities

The first thing to consider when defining the concept of indigenous peoples is whether they have Self-identification. So self-identification is regarded as a fundamental criterion for determining whether a particular group is indigenous. In addition, under the assumption that the above conditions are met International law does identify certain characteristics of Indigenous Peoples as below (Article 1, ILO Convention 169 on Indigenous and Tribal Peoples states, 1989);

> *"Peoples in independent countries who are regarded as indigenous on account of their descent from the populations which inhabited the country, or a geographical region to which the country belongs, at the time of conquest or colonization or the establishment of present state boundaries and who, irrespective of their legal status, retain some or all of their own social, economic, cultural and political institutions."*

In 2003, detailed characteristics of Indigenous Peoples were embodied. According to The Manual for the Convention 169 (2003), indigenous peoples have four characteristics:

- *traditional life styles*
- *culture and way of life different from the other segments of the national population; for example, in their ways of making a living, language, customs, etc.*
- *own social organization and political institutions*
- *living in historical continuity in a certain area, or before others 'invaded' or came to the area*

Although there is no precise definition of 'minority' in international law, the UN system recognizes national or ethnic, religious and linguistic minorities and the right of persons belonging to these groups to enjoy their own culture, to profess and practice their own religion, and to use their own language (Article 27 of the International Covenant on Civil and Political Rights; Article 2 of the UN Declaration on the Rights of Persons Belonging to National or Ethnic, Religious and Linguistic Minorities).

While Article 27 identifies to which minorities the article applies, it offers no explanation as to what defines a 'minority.' Any single definition would likely not capture the breadth of diverse minority groups that exist worldwide. However, certain common characteristics can be identified. In particular, minority groups often share the following:

- a non-dominant or marginalized position, relative to the rest of the population
- ethnic, religious or linguistic characteristics distinct from those of the rest

of the population
- a desire to preserve their distinct culture, traditions, language and religion

In terms of enhancing ethnic minority's right, the UN Declaration on the Rights of Indigenous Peoples was adopted in 2007. Furthermore, since 2008, in UN Human Rights Council, the rights for indigenous peoples were covered.

2. Concept of the indigenous minority peoples in Russia

Apart from the above international definition of the Indigenous Minority Peoples, the Russian Federal Law identifies Indigenous Small Peoples. The Russian Federation is a multinational country, which includes many ethnic groups living in Russia. Ethnic groups that live in Russia are usually divided into four groups in Russian legal literature: Titular Nation Russians, Titular Nations in Republics, Indigenous Minority Peoples and National Minorities.

According to the Article 1 of the Russian federal law № 83-FL (On guaranties of the rights of Indigenous Small Peoples in the Russian Federation 1999), Indigenous Minority Peoples of the Russian Federation, these peoples fulfil the four requirements. They must live in their historical territory and they preserve their traditional way of life, occupations, and trades. Of course, they must recognize themselves as a separate ethnicity and also have at most 50.000 of their population within

Russia.

The following peoples in the <Table 1> are officially recognized minor indigenous peoples of Russia. Many of them are included into the Common List of Minor Indigenous Peoples of Russia (Единый перечень коренных малочисленных народов России) approved by the government of Russia on March 24, 2000.

<Table 1> The unified List of the Indigenous Minority Peoples in Russia

Far North (The part of Russia which lies mainly beyond the Arctic Circle)		
Ainus (Айны)	Aleuts (Алеуты)	Alyutors (Алюторцы)
Chukchis (чукчи)	Chuvans (чуванцы)	Dolgans (долганы)
Enets (энцы)	Siberian Yupik (Yuit, Yupigyt, эскимосы)	Itelmens (ительмены)
Kamchadals (камчадалы)	Kereks (кереки)	Komi peoples (Коми-ижемцы)
Koryaks (коряки)	Nenets (ненцы)	Nganasans (нганасаны)
Sami (саамы, саамы)	Veps (вепсы)	Yukaghirs (юкагиры)
Central Siberia		
Chulyms (чулымцы)	Evenks (эвенки)	Evens (эвены)
Kets (кеты)	Khantys (ханты)	Mansi (манси)
Selkups (селькупы)	Teleuts (телеуты)	
Far East		
Nanais (нанайцы)	Negidals (негидальцы)	Nivkh people (нивхи)
Oroch people (орочи)	Orok people (Ulta, Uilta, ороки, ульта)	Taz people (тазы)
Udege people (удэгейцы)	Ulch people (ульчи)	
Southern Siberia		
Kumandins (кумандинцы)	Chelkans (челканцы)	Shorians (шорцы)
Soyots (сойоты)	Telengits (теленгиты)	Tofalars (тофалары)
Tubalars (тубалары)	Tuvans-Todzhins (тувинцы-тоджинцы)	
Other		
Abazins (абазины)	Besermyan (бесермяне)	Izhorians (ижорцы)
Nagaybaks (нагайбаки)	Votes (ВОДЬ)	Seto (Сету, сето)

Source: Document "Unified List of the Indigenous Minority Peoples in Russia" (March, 2000)

The list has increased in number since the Soviet period and includes more than 40 Peoples. As a result, the total population increased by 30,000 from the Soviet period record. The concept of indigenous minorities that Russian government does define has a similar context in the framework of international definitions mentioned above. However, one big difference is that it does not define the concept of indigenous peoples. Russia defines the concept of "Indigenous small peoples" or "Small ethnic communities" instead of the concept of indigenous peoples.

It is true that the concept of indigenous peoples and ethnic minorities in Russia has been used without strict distinction even in academic papers and the media. This is due to the concept of indigenous peoples living on the land where their ancestors had lived before the influence of Russia. Because they have fewer people than Russians so because of this fact in Russian society, the effect of identifying minorities and indigenous peoples is common. However, "Indigenous peoples" and "Ethnic minorities" – these two concepts need to be clearly distinguished because there are various ethnic groups not only who lived in Russian territory before Russia's influence (They are called indigenous peoples), but also who migrated to and settled in Russia long ago by historical reasons.

3. Status of the indigenous minority peoples in Russia

Since the last census of the Soviet period in 1989, Russia has conducted a total of two Russia-Wide Census in 2002 and 2010 until 2019 called "All-Russian Census (Всероссийская перепись населения)" According to the 2010 Russian Census, there are 273,990 indigenous monority peoples living in all Russian territories, of which 215,847 are the nationally recognized 'Indigenous monority peoples in northern Russia.' The rest are indigenous monority peoples living in western Russia.

In terms of the number of people in each race, the most populous are the Nenets (44,640) and the least populous are the Kereks (4). (All-Russian Census, 2010) Socolova and Stefanov based on the 2002 census, divided minority groups into three groups by population. The first group contains less than 50,000 people. They show a demographically stable form, with no significant decrease or increase in numbers. The first group accounts for about 80% of the total population of Russian indigenous minorities. The nations belonging to the first group include the Nenets, Mansi, and Khanty. The second group is ethnic groups with populations ranging from 10,000 to 1,000, including Hicks, Dolgans and Itelmenians. The third group is ethnic groups with a hundred or ten population, such as the Oroch and Enets. This trend is similar in the 2010 census (Hye Jin Kim 2012, 55)

<Table 2> Population change of the Indigenous Minority Peoples in Russia

(Unit: Person)

		The result of Census 1989	The result of Census 2002	The result of Census 2010
1	Aleut (АЛЕУТЫ)	700	540	482
2	Vepsians (ВЕПСЫ)	13000	8240	5936
3	Dolgans (ДОЛГАНЫ)	6900	7261	7885
4	Itelmens (ИТЕЛЬМЕНЫ)	2500	3180	3193
5	Ket (КЕТЫ)	1100	1494	1219
6	Koryaks (КОРЯКИ)	9200	8743	7953
7	Mansi (МАНСИ)	8500	11432	12269
8	Nanai (НАНАЙЦЫ)	12000	12160	12003
9	Nganasans НГАНАСАНЫ)	1300	834	862
10	Negidals (НЕГИДАЛЬЦЫ)	600	567	513
11	Nenets(НЕНЦЫ)	35000	41302	44640
12	Nivkhi (НИВХИ)	4700	5162	4652
13	Oroch(ОРОЧИ)	200	686	596
14	Sami (СААМЫ)	1900	1991	1771
15	Selkup (СЕЛЬКУПЫ)	3600	4249	3649
16	Teleuts (ТЕЛЕУТЫ)		2650	2643
17	Tofalars(Tofa) (ТОФАЛАРЫ (ТОФА))	700	837	762
18	Udeghes (УДЭГЕЙЦЫ)	2000	1657	1496
19	Uiltas(Orok) (УЙЛЬТА(ОРОКИ))	200	346	295
20	Ulchs (УЛЬЧИ)	3200	2913	2765
21	Khanty (ХАНТЫ)	23000	28678	30943
22	Chuvans (ЧУВАНЦЫ)	1500	1087	1002
23	Chukchi (ЧУКЧИ)	15000	15765	15908
24	Shors (ШОРЦЫ)	17000	13975	12888
25	Evenks (ЭВЕНКИ)	30000	35527	37843
26	Evens(Lamuts) (ЭВЕНЫ (ЛАМУТЫ))	17000	19071	22383
27	Enets (ЭНЦЫ)	200	237	227
28	Eskimo (ЭСКИМОСЫ)	1700	1750	1738
29	Yukaghir (ЮКАГИРЫ)	1100	1509	1603

Source: This table is written by author based on the results of the Soviet Union's 1989 census and 2002 and 2010 Russian census and of the 47 indigenous minority peoples, only 29 ethnic groups were mentioned in all three census.

Indigenous minority peoples in northern Russia is important to the Russian government. The first reason is the statistical values that are primarily visible. As mentioned earlier, most of Russia's indigenous minority peoples live in the northern regions. The second reason is from economic reasons. Northern Russia, where most of the indigenous minorities live, is home to more than 60 percent of Russia's mineral resources surveyed and more than half of its fur and leather. In addition, 90% of natural gas produced in Russia, 75% of oil, 15% of coal, and other significant amounts of jewels such as nickel, gold, copper, tin, and diamonds are collected from this region (Trafimov 2007, 8).

In other words, the share of northern Russia in the Russian economy is strong. The nationalist craze that began in the late 1980s extended to northern Russia. Minorities have also begun to voice their voices, and even the government has to pay attention to minorities in order to prevent ethnic conflicts or separation.

The economic activities of the indigenous minority peoples in this country are characterized by their traditional livelihoods from their ancestors, far from urbanization and industrialization. The traditional economic activities of them can be divided into several categories:

- *reindeer breeding, horse breeding, rearing, etc. and processing of fur, leather, bone, heel, horn, meat, etc. obtained from the animals;*
- *dog breeding (for hunting or moving purposes);*

- *beekeeping;*
- *fishing;*
- *hunting;*
- *agriculture and vegetable cultivation;*
- *forestry;*
- *Various harvesting businesses and processing of harvested fruits and herbs.*

Of course, unlike in the past, many changes have occurred, such as the introduction of new technologies and machines, such as helicopters and motor boats, into their economic activities. However, their traditional economic activities are traditional livelihoods, as traditional territories (or catching areas) and their sectors continue to this day. However, not all indigenous minority peoples are engaged in a living inherited from their ancestral territories. The level of urbanization is growing among indigenous ethnic minorities.

III. International and domestic legislation for the indigenous minority peoples in Russia

1. International commitments and legal regulation in Russia

There have been some achievements in the field of indigenous people's rights at the international level. The Permanent Forum on

Indigenous Issues was created and has been working since 2002 (The official website of the Forum, April 2014). The Second Decade of Indigenous Peoples was declared by the United Nations from 2005 to 2014 (The UN General Assembly Resolution A/RES//59/174, December 22, 2004) and the UN General Assembly Resolution A/60/270/ADD.1, August 26, 2005).

The UN Declaration on Rights of Indigenous Peoples was adopted, and the Expert Mechanism on the Rights of Indigenous Peoples was established by the UN Human Rights Council and began its work in 2008. The UN Forum became a place where representatives of indigenous peoples from different parts of our Planet meet and discuss their problems and exchange their experiences with each other and can ask questions to the governments and international organizations. At the end of each session, advice and recommendations are given to the UN Economic and Social Council (ECOSOC).

Russian indigenous minority peoples are also represented at the Forum and their voice could be heard at the international level. Russia began ratifying international law and joying international activities on the protection of the indigenous minority peoples since the days of the Soviet Union. In 1969 the Soviet Union, ratified the UN International Convention on the Elimination of All Forms of Racial Discrimination and it ratified the two main UN human rights treaties – the International Covenant on Civil and Political Rights and the International Covenant on Economic, Social and Cultural

Rights in 1973. In 1996, the Russian Federation became a member of the Council of Europe, and it ratified both the European Convention on Human Rights (ECHR) and the Framework Convention for the Protection of National Minorities (FCNM) in 1998. When it acceded to the Council of Europe, Russia also committed to become a state party to the European Charter for Regional or Minority Languages; however, although it signed the Charter in 2001, ratification was still pending at the time of writing.

After joining the Council of Europe, Russia initiated a process of legal reform, involving the adoption of new criminal and civil provisions. Article 15(4) of the Constitution declares the supremacy of international law over Russian law. The article states as below:

> *"The universally-recognized norms of international law and international treaties and agreements of the Russian Federation shall be a component part of its legal system. If an international treaty or agreement of the Russian Federation establishes other rules than those envisaged by law, the rules of the international agreement shall be applied."*

The present Federal Law in accordance with the Constitution of the Russian Federation, the conventional principles and regulations of international law and international treaties of the Russian Federation shall determine the legal foundations of guarantees of the unique social, economic and cultural development of indigenous small-numbered peoples of the Russian Federation, protection of their native habitat, traditional way of life, economic activities and crafts.

Looking at the following article in the Russian Constitution, it can be seen that the Russian Federation law relating to indigenous minority people protection law is in line with international law. The article 69 of Constitution of the Russian Federation (1993) shows that the Russian Federation shall guarantee the rights of the indigenous minority peoples according to the universally recognized principles and norms of international law and international treaties and agreements of the Russian Federation as below;

> *"The Russian Federation shall guarantee the rights of the indigenous minority peoples according to the universally recognized principles and norms of international law and international treaties and agreements of the Russian Federation."*

Although the Russian Constitution like the article 69 guarantees the rights of the indigenous minority peoples according to the universally recognized principles and norms of international law and international agreements, it does not mean that there are real international guaranties to the rights of the indigenous minority peoples exist in Russia in line with international law. Because Russia refused to ratify the ILO Convention № 169 (1989) and abstained from signing the UN Declaration on Rights of Indigenous Peoples (2007). Since Russia still has not ratified ILO Convention № 169 and has not supported the UN Declaration on Rights of Indigenous Peoples, there are no real international legal guarantees for indigenous minorities concerning mining activity on their lands.

2. Domestic legislation for the indigenous minority peoples in Russia

The Russian national law is quite specific, diverse and, at the same time, very fragmented with regard to the rights and interests of indigenous peoples. There are many laws and normative legal acts affecting various aspects of life and activities of indigenous communities and their representatives. It is worth highlighting Article 69 and 72 of Russian Constitution, which refers to the joint regulation of the rights and freedoms of national minorities by regions and the federation. According to the 2 articles (Article 69 and 72) of the Russian Constitutional Law directly applied to the indigenous minority people as below;

Article 69

"The Russian Federation shall guarantee the rights of the indigenous minority peoples according to the universally recognized principles and norms of international law and international treaties and agreements of the Russian Federation."

Article 72

"The joint jurisdiction of the Russian Federation and the subjects of the Russian Federation includes protection of traditional living habitat and of traditional way of life of small ethnic communities."

Going specific, there are three categories of basic Federal Laws about the rights of indigenous peoples; 1) On the Guarantees of the Rights of the Indigenous Small-numbered Peoples of the Russian Federation (The federal law № 83-FL); 2) On General Principles of Organization the Indigenous Small-numbered Peoples' Communities of the North, Siberia and Far East of the Russian Federation (The federal law № 104-FL); and 3) On Territories of Traditional Land Use of the Indigenous Small-numbered Peoples of the North, Siberia and the Far East of the Russian Federation (The federal law № 49-FL).

2.1. The Federal Law № 83-FL: On the guarantees of the rights of the indigenous small-numbered peoples of the Russian federation

As mentioned earlier when defining the concept of indigenous minorities in Russia, the Russian government defines the basic concepts of indigenous minorities, their categories and their basic rights through the following provisions of law. The author analyzed the provisions of this law into three major themes: "Definitions of 'indigenous small peoples,'" "Legal sphere of the law" and "Basic rights of indigenous small peoples."

Firstly, basic concepts of 'indigenous small peoples'; In article 1 (1) the Russian Federation law defines "Definitions of indigenous small people." By the concept of the Russian federal law, "Indigenous small peoples" – are peoples who live on the traditional territories of their ancestors, keeping their ancient lifestyle, habitat, activity, numbering not more than 50 thousand of members in the Russian Federation and recognize themselves as independent ethnic communities." In addition, article 1 defines 'traditional way of life,' 'native habitat,' 'communities and other forms of public self-government,' 'authorized representatives' and 'ethnological analysis.'

The thing to watch out for here is that the Russian legislation does not contain the concept of «indigenous people», the definition of which appears in ILO Convention No. 169 (1989). Russia is not a party to international treaties on the rights of indigenous peoples, since it has its own political and legal strategy in the field of national ethno-politics. It is also important to note that disputes about inclusion in the Government List of various ethnic groups arise periodically in the Russian public and legal sphere. These disputes are caused by the fact that the «mechanism» of assigning an ethnic group to «indigenous small-numbered peoples» is unclear.

Secondly, the part of the legal sphere of the law; the Russian federal law does define the legal sphere of the law in three categories:

1) indigenous small peoples; 2) individuals from indigenous communities and for whom traditional activity is ancillary, but no the basic; and 3) individuals who live on traditional territories of indigenous small peoples.

The first category is "true indigenous people," who live on the lands of their ancestors from time immemorial, are not going to change their way of life, trying to preserve and pass on to their children the experience of generations, ignoring the trends of urbanized society. This category includes those who live in the tundra, forest-tundra, taiga, etc. The second category is indigenous people, for whom traditional lifestyle is only an additional kind of household. They also recognize themselves as independent ethnic groups, and live in the regions. The third category is the population that is not included in the Unified Federal List of Indigenous Small-Numbered Peoples, but permanently resides in places of their traditional residence and traditional economic activities, and has similar way of life.

Finally, basic rights of indigenous small peoples; the Russian federal law guarantees the native habitats, traditional way of life, economic activities and crafts of indigenous peoples, indigenous communities and persons designated as indigenous people. The rights of ethnic minorities officially established by the state can be largely divided into the following political, economic, and social cultural areas.

Political aspects:

- *Minorities can participate in the administration of national power authorities and municipalities.*
- *Minorities can organize special constituencies and national dwellings with small populations and organize ethnic groups.*
- *Minorities and their communities can participate in environmental sentiment on their traditional territories.*
- *Special quotas will be set up for representatives of ethnic minorities within national institutions.*

Economic aspects:

- *Territory is protected by the state, which can be applied to the traditional methods of natural use of minorities.*
- *Where officially designated as a special territory of ethnic minorities, prohibit any industrial activities that may cause environmental pollution.*
- *As part of traditional economic development, a budget for folk crafts is allocated.*
- *Regard to the interests of indigenous peoples, manufacturing enterprises may be subject to privatization. At the same time, taxation of such enterprises will be carried out taking into account possible benefits and subsidies.*
- *Companies which are associated with traditional economic activities of minority groups and their territories provide subsidies and other benefits to minorities.*

Sociocultural aspects:

- *Supports the preserving of ethnic language and ethnic culture.*
- *Periodically supports the scientific research on the cultural spheres of the minorities.*

- *Introduce national and regional elements to national education standards.*
- *Replace military service with another service.*
- *Support public health services at low cost.*

2.2. The Federal Law № 104-FL: On general principles of organization the indigenous small-numbered peoples' communities of the North, Siberia and Far East of the Russian Federation

There are six categories of basic concepts of small-numbered indigenous peoples of the North, Siberia and Far East of the Russian Federation; Representatives of other ethnic communities; Communities of small-numbered peoples; Family (tribal) communities of indigenous peoples; Territorial and neighboring communities of indigenous peoples; and Unions (associations) of communities of indigenous peoples. The Russian law regulates the legal status of 47 indigenous small-numbered peoples, 40 of them belong to the small-numbered indigenous peoples of the North, Siberia and the Far East of the Russian Federation.

The federal law № 104-FL and № 49-FL provide essential principles of indigenous communities (organizational structure, constituent documents, number of members and etc.) and the legal regime of traditional territories of indigenous small peoples (legal and formal procedure of foundation). The present Federal law № 104-FL determines the general principles of organization and activities of small-numbered peoples of the North, Siberia and Far East of the Russian Federation for protecting territories of traditional nature use of the indigenous small-numbered peoples, rights and legal interests of mentioned indigenous peoples as well as establishes the legal basis of communal forms of self-government and state guarantees for its implementation.

2.3. The Federal Law № 49-FL: On territories of traditional land use of the indigenous small-numbered peoples of the North, Siberia and the Far East of the Russian Federation

The present Federal Law determines the legal principles of the establishment, protection and operation of the territories of traditional land use of the indigenous small-numbered peoples of the North, Siberia and Far East of the Russian Federation for keeping within these territories traditional way of life.

Then, several basic concepts are used in the present Federal Law. For example, the territories of traditional land use of the indigenous small-numbered peoples of the North, Siberia and the Far East of the Russian Federation are specially protected wildlife areas established for the purposes of traditional land use and traditional way of life of the indigenous small-numbered peoples of the North, Siberia and the Far East of the Russian Federation.

Traditional land use of the indigenous small-numbered peoples of the North, Siberia and the Far East of the Russian Federation is historically formed and providing sustainable environmental development methods of operating objects of the flora and fauna and other natural resources by indigenous small-numbered peoples of the North, Siberia and the Far East of the Russian Federation. Customs of the indigenous small-numbered peoples of the North, Siberia and the Far East of the Russian Federation are traditionally formed and widely-used by indigenous small-numbered peoples of the North, Siberia and the Far East of the Russian Federation rules.

3. Limitations and problems of the policies for the indigenous minority peoples in Russia

According to the Russian Federal Law about Guarantees of the Rights of Indigenous Minority Peoples of the Russian Federation, these peoples have the right to protect their lands and traditional way of life. Provisions were adopted for ecological and ethnological examination before any resource extraction on the lands of indigenous minority peoples. However, these provisions still do not work, because the mechanism for such examinations has not yet been established. Therefore, these standards exist only on paper, but not in reality.

The fact that the Russian government has adopted a number of laws related to ethnic minorities suggests that the government recognizes their legitimate rights to their own territories and autonomy. Russia's indigenous minority policy aims to guarantee the rights of indigenous minority peoples in the political, economic and socio-cultural aspects, but even after a long time since the legal basis was laid, there is still a lot of controversy and limitations like conflicts with other laws and lack of consistency before and after amendment.

The Federal Law about Territories of Traditional Natural Resource Use of the Indigenous Minorities of the North, Siberia and the Far East of the Russian Federation (Russian Federal Law on the Territories of Traditional Nature Use of the Indigenous Minorities of the North, Siberia and the Far East of the Russian Federation, 2001) does not resolve the problem either. Even though indigenous minority peoples have been living in the Northern territories of the Russian Federation for ages de-facto, they cannot confirm their right to the land de-jure.

Consequently, this law contradicts to the Federal Land Code, that is why there were not created any territories of traditional natural resource use for indigenous minority peoples at the federal level. Although the Constitution of the Russian Federation articles and the Federal Laws set the basic legal system for the protection of the rights of indigenous minority peoples in the Russian Federation, this system is full of legal gaps and contradictions, and has to be developed according to international standards. Furthermore, the statutes sometimes may lose its consistency before and after the revision. For example, the Fishery and Water Protection Act (Закон о рыболовстве и сохранении водынх биологических ресурсов), enacted in 2004, was amended in 2008, which abolished legislation that provided free fishing areas to the indigenous minority peoples and their communities.

Moreover, the "Environmental Appraisal Act" enacted in 1995 also had many problems. The Environmental Appraisal Act specifies that national environmental appraisal procedures should be followed to understand the impact of business activities on the surrounding environment. This was to protect the territorial and environmental protections of indigenous minority peoples. However, the problem has been revealed in the process of national appreciation, reflecting the subjectivity of experts, lack of long-term monitoring, and the activities and influence of pro-business lobbyists (Hye Jin Kim 2012, 65).

Another problem is that legislation is not being implemented properly. In the 10 years since the law was enacted, the "Territorial Law about traditional resource utilization" has never actually been designated as a minority territory at the federal level. Even at the federal level, the law is ineffective, so it is hard to expect legal effect in the district court. For example, in 2006, the State of Irkutsk and Ebenk Autonomous Regions the ruling was declined to provide "traditional resource use territory" to indigenous minorities in the region. (Novikova 2008, 28). In the case of such a conflict between commercial interests and minority interests and environmental protection, it is not uncommon for the court to rule over substantive economic gains over minorities.

From the point of view of the administrative entities that make up the Russian Federation, attracting large corporations is an important factor for regional economic development. Therefore, it is more likely to be on the side of large corporations than to protect the rights of Indigenous minorities. As such, while the Russian government is trying to protect its Indigenous minority through various legislation, it can be seen that it has many problems and limitations.

There is no doubt that the Russian government legally protects the rights of indigenous minorities and minorities and encourage and support them to live rooted in society. It is also true that within the legal framework that protects them, practical and material support is also provided to protect their culture, language and living conditions. Nevertheless, as mentioned earlier, indigenous peoples, minorities, the Russian federal law that protects them but not the social majority.

IV. Conclusion

There are almost no absolutely homogeneous countries in the 21th century. This in turn increases the value of the ethnic component in modern politics. Ethnic diversity has always been a potential conflict factor and a source of political instability. Therefore, the national question is of particular importance for almost all states in the world. Each country has developed its own set of measures for the regulation of inter-ethnic relations, whether it is the support of ethnic political parties or reserved seats for ethnic groups, ethnic quotas or the creation of institutions of ethnic representation.

The concept of indigenous minorities that Russian government defines has a similar context in the framework of international definitions mentioned above. However, one big difference is that it does not define the concept of indigenous peoples. Russia defines the concept of "Indigenous small peoples" or "Small ethnic communities" instead of the concept of indigenous peoples. "Indigenous peoples" and "Ethnic minorities" – these two concepts need to be clearly distinguished because there are various ethnic groups not only who lived in the Russian territory before Russia's influence (They are called indigenous peoples), but also who migrated to and settled in Russia long ago by historical reasons.

Russia, despite various controversies, cannot deny the fact that it is working to protect the rights of ethnic minorities. The ethnic minority policy of the Russian state has caused many problems and controversies, but it must be contributing to the strengthening of the ethnic minority's identity and the protection of the minority. Now, as many peoples want to be recognized as ethnic minorities, Russia is facing the task of scrutinizing and reviewing indigenous minority policies. The Russian culture and the Russian language are solidifying their foundations as a foundational culture of society through the period of Imperial Russian and Soviet Union. Furthermore, it is also true that along with these attempts policies co-exist to protect the cultural rights of individual minorities and non-native peoples.

It is pretty difficult to identify a universal set of factors that are effective for the political representation of ethnic groups in each country. One thing is clear that, despite significant differences, all states should not lose sight of the issues of ethnic nature; there is also need for constant monitoring of inter-ethnic situation, improvement of legislation in this area, an analysis of the international situation, collective methods of work at the regional scale and promotion of patriotic and civic education and much more.

Reference

Hye Jin Kim. "Ethnic minorities in Russia and Russian policy, Center for Internationa Area Studies" *Journal of international area studies,* Vol. 16, No. 1 (2012).

Kharyuchi Sergey Nikolayevich. "Development of legislation on the protection of the rights of indigenous small peoples in the Russian federation" *Journal of Russian Law* ,Vol. 7, No. 115 13-22 (2006).

Novikova. N.I, "Oil Law and Aboriginal Rights" *Ethnographic Review*, No. 3. 28-36 (2008).

Maksim Zadorin, Olga Klisheva, Ksenia Vezhlivtsevam, Daria Antufieva. "Russian Laws on Indigenous Issues. Guarantees, Communities, Territories of Traditional Land Use: Translated and commented" *University of Lapland Rovaniemi* (2017).

McGarry, John. "Demographic engineering: The state-directed movement of ethnic groups as a technique of conflict regulation" *Ethnic and Racial Studies* 21 (1998).

Sokolova, Stepanov. "Indigenous Peoples of the North. Population dynamics according to censuses" *Ethnographic Review*, No.5 (2007).

Trofimov. E. "The main directions of forming the legislative base of national policy" *Vlast',* No. 5 (2007).

Tishkov, Valerii. "Ethnicity, Nationalism and Conflict in and after the Soviet Union: the Mind Aflame," *London: Sage Publication* (1997).

All-Soviet Union Population Census 1989 (Vsesoyuznaya perepis' naseleniya 1989 г.)

All-Russian Population Census 2002 (Vsesoyuznaya perepis' naseleniya 2002 г.)

All-Russian Population Census 2010 (Vsesoyuznaya perepis' naseleniya 2010 г)

On the Guarantees of the Rights of the Indigenous Small-numbered Peoples of the Russian Federation (The federal law № 83-FL), Official site of the